THE AUTHOR

Wilfred Owen was born at Plas Wilmot, Oswestry, Shropshire in 1893, the eldest of the four children of Tom Owen, a railway official, and his wife Susan – to whom Wilfred was devoted all his life. He spent most of his childhood in Birkenhead but in 1906 the family moved to Shrewsbury where he was educated at the Technical School. On failing to win a scholarship to London University in 1911 he accepted an appointment as assistant to the vicar of Dunsden, near Reading. Eighteen months later, he again failed to win a scholarship, to University College, Reading. As a result of this set-back, a crisis in his relations with the vicar, and a subsequent illness, he decided to go to France, and there teach English at the Berlitz School of Languages in Bordeaux. He returned to England in 1915 and joined up in the Artists' Rifles, embarking to fight in France the following winter as an officer in the Manchester Regiment. In May 1917 he was evacuated from the front line suffering from shellshock. During four months at Craiglockhart hospital, Edinburgh, he met Siegfried Sassoon and Robert Graves. In 1918 five of his poems were published – the only five he was to see in print, for that autumn he returned to the front, where, in October, he won the Military Cross. He was killed one week before the Armistice while attempting to move his company of the 2nd Manchesters across the Oise and Sambre Canal near Ors.

Owen's poetry is known throughout the English-speaking world, and indeed beyond it as the text of Benjamin Britten's *War Requiem*. Sassoon's edition of his poems was published in 1920, Edmund Blunden's in 1931, C. Day Lewis's in 1963, Dominic Hibberd's in 1973, and *The Collected Letters*, edited by Harold Owen and John Bell, in 1967. This new, authoritative edition of the poems, derives from the two-volume *Complete Poems and Fragments*, published in 1983, which made available more than twice the number of poems and fragments previously in print.

Preface.

This book is not about heroes. English Poetry
is not yet fit to speak of them.
Nor is it about battles, and glory of battles, and lands,
about glory, honour,
nor anything about
might, majesty, dominion or power
except War.

Above all this Book is not concerned with Poetry.
The subject of it is War, and the pity of War.
The Poetry is in the pity.

Yet these elegies are not to this generation,
this is in no sense consolatory
to this generation. They may be to the
next.

All a Poet can do today is warn. That is why the True War Poet must be truthful.

If I thought the letter of this book would last,
I might have used proper names; but if the spirit of
it survives Prussia, — my ambition and these names will
be content; for they will have achieved themselves fresher fields than Flanders,
for be, out of war,

would be

THE POEMS
OF
WILFRED
OWEN

Edited and Introduced by
Jon Stallworthy

THE HOGARTH PRESS
LONDON

Published in 1985 by
The Hogarth Press
40 William IV Street, London WC2N 4DF

The Poems and Fragments of Wilfred Owen
© The Executors of Harold Owen's Estate 1963 and 1983
Foreword, Biographical Table, Introduction, List of
Abbreviations and Notes
© Jon Stallworthy 1985
'Two Fusiliers', p. 102, by Robert Graves
© Robert Graves

British Library Cataloguing in Publication Data

Owen, Wilfred
The poems of Wilfred Owen.
I. Title
821'912   PR6029.W4
ISBN 0 7012 1015 X

Phototypeset by
Wyvern Typesetting Limited, Bristol

Printed in Great Britain by
Cox & Wyman Ltd
Reading, Berkshire

FOREWORD

This edition makes available to the student and general reader the texts and notes of 103 poems and 12 fragments published in the two-volume *Complete Poems and Fragments* (1983). That work sought to establish the texts and the chronology of all Owen's surviving poems and fragments, to chart their manuscripts, and to offer such factual (as distinct from interpretative) notes as the reader might need to understand them. In that endeavour, it built upon foundations laid by previous editors – Mr Siegfried Sassoon (assisted by Dame Edith Sitwell), Professor Edmund Blunden, Mr Cecil Day Lewis, and Dr Dominic Hibberd – to the last of whom I owed a particular debt. Dr Hibberd had been at work on a critical study of Owen's poems while I was editing the texts, and he was more than generous in sharing his solutions of our common problems.

Editions of this kind necessarily bring together the work and insights of many people, and I should like to record especial gratitude to the editors of the *Collected Letters*, Mr John Bell and the late Harold Owen, Dr Cathrael Kazin who transcribed and dated many of the manuscripts, Miss Catharine Carver the paragon of publishers' editors, and, last but not least, my wife who so good naturedly and for so long accepted Wilfred Owen as a ghostly addition to the family.

Cornell University   J.H.S.
Ithaca, New York
October 1984

CONTENTS

Biographical Table: Wilfred Owen 1893–1918 xi
Introduction xix
List of Abbreviations xxiv

THE POEMS
To Poesy 3
Written in a Wood, September 1910 7
Sonnet / Written at Teignmouth, on a Pilgrimage
    to Keats's House 8
Lines Written on My Nineteenth Birthday 9
Supposed Confessions of a Secondrate Sensitive
    Mind in Dejection 11
The Dread of Falling into Naught 14
Science has looked 15
The Little Mermaid 17
The Two Reflections 38
Deep under turfy grass 39
Unto what pinnacles 40
Sonnet / Daily I muse on her 41
Uriconium 42
When late I viewed the gardens 46
Long ages past 47
O World of many worlds 48
The time was aeon 50
Nocturne 52
Impromptu / Now, let me feel 53
A Palinode 54
It was a navy boy 56
Whereas most women live 58
A New Heaven 59
Storm 60
To the Bitter Sweet-Heart: A Dream 61
Roundel / In Shrewsbury Town 62
How Do I Love Thee? 63
The Fates 64
Happiness 65
Song of Songs 66
Has your soul sipped 67

The Swift 69
Inspection 72
With an Identity Disc 73
The Promisers 74
Music 75
Anthem for Doomed Youth 76
Winter Song 78
Six O'clock in Princes Street 79
The One Remains 80
The Sleeping Beauty 81
The city lights 82
Autumnal 83
The Unreturning 84
Perversity 85
Maundy Thursday 86
The Peril of Love 87
The Poet in Pain 88
Whither is passed 89
On My Songs 90
To —— 91
To Eros 92
1914 93
Purple 94
On a Dream 95
Stunned by their life's explosion 96
From My Diary, July 1914 97
The Ballad of Many Thorns 98
I saw his round mouth's crimson 100
Apologia pro Poemate Meo 101
Le Christianisme 103
Hospital Barge 104
Sweet is your antique body 106
Page Eglantine 107
The Rime of the Youthful Mariner 108
Who is the god of Canongate? 109
My Shy Hand 110
At a Calvary near the Ancre 111
Miners 112
The Letter 114
Conscious 115

Schoolmistress 116
Dulce et Decorum Est 117
A Tear Song 119
The Dead-Beat 121
Insensibility 122
Strange Meeting 125
Sonnet/On Seeing a Piece of Our Heavy Artillery
    Brought into Action 128
Asleep 129
Arms and the Boy 131
The Show 132
Futility 135
The End 136
S.I.W. 137
The Calls 139
Training 141
The Next War 142
Greater Love 143
The Last Laugh 145
Mental Cases 146
The Chances 148
The Send-Off 149
The Parable of the Old Man and the Young 151
Disabled 152
A Terre 155
The Kind Ghosts 158
Soldier's Dream 159
I am the ghost of Shadwell Stair 160
Elegy in April and September 161
Exposure 162
The Sentry 165
Smile, Smile, Smile 167
Spring Offensive 169

THE FRAGMENTS
Full springs of Thought around me rise 175
An Imperial Elegy 177
I know the music 178
But I was looking at the permanent stars 179
Beauty 180

Spells and Incantation 181
Cramped in that funnelled hole 183
The Wrestlers 184
Wild with All Regrets 188
As bronze may be much beautified 190
The roads also 191
Owen's Preface 192

Index of titles and first lines 193

Frontispiece
Owen's draft Preface (reproduced by permission of the British Library).
See p. 192 for a transcription.

Dates of composition and revision will be found under
the texts of individual poems

1893 *18 March* Wilfred Edward Salter Owen (WO) born at Plas
Wilmot, Oswestry, son of Tom and Susan Owen

1895 *30 May* Mary Millard Owen born

1897 *16 March* Plas Wilmot sold at Grandfather Shaw's death.
Tom Owen appointed to supervisory post at Birkenhead with
the Great Western and London and North Eastern Railways
April Tom Owen applies for transfer; appointed to
Shrewsbury
5 September Harold Owen (HO) born in Canon Street,
Shrewsbury

1897-8 *Winter* Tom Owen reappointed to Birkenhead. Family moves
to 14 Willmer Road, Birkenhead

1898 *Spring* Holiday in Ireland

1898-9 Move to 7 Elm Grove, Birkenhead, and further move to 51
Milton Street, Birkenhead

1900 *11 June* WO starts school (in mid-term) at the Birkenhead
Institute
24 July Colin Shaw Owen (CO) born

1902 *Summer* Holiday at Tramore, Ireland

1903
or *Summer* Holiday in Broxton
1904

1905 *Summer* Holiday in Scarborough
August Holiday with the Paton family at Rhewl, Wales

1906 *July* Holiday at Torquay and Carbis Bay
Summer Holiday with the Smallpage family at Waenfawr,
Wales

1906-7 *Winter* Tom Owen appointed Assistant Superintendent, GW
and LNER, Western Region; the family moves to 1 Cleveland
Place, Underdale Road, Shrewsbury. WO starts at
Shrewsbury Technical School

1908 *April* WO stays with the Gunston family in Wimbledon
June Tom Owen takes WO to Brittany

1909 *July* WO goes again to Brittany with his father, then to
Torquay

1910 *January* The family moves to Mahim, Monkmoor Road, Shrewsbury

August WO and HO on holiday in Torquay. WO calls on Miss Christabel Coleridge, granddaughter of the poet

1911 *April* WO again on holiday in Torquay; reads Sidney Colvin's *Keats* and visits Teignmouth

Summer Works as a pupil-teacher at the Wyle Cop School, Shrewsbury, while preparing for matriculation exam

9 September Takes University of London matriculation exam. Visits British Museum to see Keats manuscripts

28 September Interview with the Revd Herbert Wigan, vicar of Dunsden, near Reading. Is offered an unpaid post as lay assistant and pupil in this Evangelical parish

Early October Hears he has matriculated, but not with honours

20 October Arrives at Dunsden

1912 *16 April* Arranges to take botany classes at University College, Reading, for six hours a week

June Meets Miss Edith Morley, head of the English Department, University College

8 July Joins family at Pringle Bank, Kelso, for holiday with the Bulman family

20–25 July Attends Keswick Convention

December Miss Morley urges him to sit for a scholarship to University College, Reading, and invites him to attend her remaining classes in Old English free of charge

Christmas At Shrewsbury

28 December Visits Mr Morgan, a clergyman at Bordesley, Birmingham, and is offered another post as lay assistant, which he does not accept. Returns to Dunsden

1913 *Early January* Determines to leave Dunsden and to break with Evangelical religion

7 February Returns to Shrewsbury

February–March Ill with congestion of the lungs

13 March HO joins the Merchant Service and sails for the Mediterranean and India

18 April–3 May Convalescent holiday in Torquay. Starts to look for teaching post

16–19 May Takes the Reading University scholarship

July HO returns to England

c. 6 July Hears he has failed to win the Reading scholarship

August Holiday with Uncle Edward Quayle's family at
Dorfold, Great Meols, Cheshire
c. 15 September To Bordeaux, to teach English at the Berlitz
School of Languages. Lodges in rue Castelmoron
28 September Moves into room at 95 rue Porte Dijeaux
Mid-October Visited in Bordeaux by Tom Owen
November Ill with gastro-enteritis
1913–14 *Winter* HO again at sea in the South Atlantic, remaining at
sea, with occasional short leaves, until autumn 1916
1914 *18 March* Twenty-first birthday
25 July Gives up job at the Berlitz School
31 July To Castel Lorenzo, Bagnères-de-Bigorre, High
Pyrenees, as tutor to Mme Léger, a Berlitz pupil
4 August War declared. French government moves to
Bordeaux
c. 21 August Meets the poet Laurent Tailhade
24 August Invited by Mme Léger to go with her to Canada in
March 1915
17 September Returns to Bordeaux with the Légers, and stays
with them at 12 rue Blanc-Dutrouilh. Starts to look for pupils
as a free-lance teacher of English
7 October Moves to temporary lodgings with the family of a
pupil, Raoul Lem, at 12 rue St. Louis, Bordeaux
12 October Mme Léger leaves for Canada
19 October Moves to new lodgings at 31 rue Desfourniels
4 December Offered post as tutor to the two elder de la
Touche boys at the Châlet, Mérignac, near Bordeaux
8 December Accepts post for a month, retaining his private
pupils and going to Mérignac in the afternoons
19 December Moves to Mérignac to live at the Châlet
1915 *Early January* Channel considered unsafe. Invited to stay at
Mérignac until the spring
10 April Miss de la Touche, the boys' aunt, decides to keep
them in France and urges WO to stay
18 May To Imperial Hotel, Russell Square, London, while
carrying out a commission at the British Industries Fair for a
Bordeaux scent manufacturer, then to Shrewsbury for a short
visit
13 June Returns to Bordeaux via Le Havre and Paris. Into
new lodgings at 18 rue Beaubadat, continuing to teach the de

la Touche boys as well as his Bordeaux pupils

20 June Considers joining the Artists' Rifles in the autumn, after returning the boys to Downside School

10 July Considers joining the Italian Cavalry if he is unable to join the Artists' Rifles

31 August Gives up lodgings to return to England; persuaded to stay on three more weeks, and finds new lodgings at 1 Place St. Christoly, Bordeaux

14 September To London with Johnny and Bobbie de la Touche

15 September Sees the boys off to Downside from Paddington and goes home to Shrewsbury

21 October Joins up in the Artists' Rifles. Into lodgings at Les Lilas, 54 Tavistock Square, w.c.

27 October Meets Harold Monro at the Poetry Bookshop, 35 Devonshire Street, W.1

15 November To Hare Hall Camp, Gidea Park, Essex, as Cadet Owen, Artists' Rifles

1916 *c. 1 January* Home on a week's leave

27 February–5 March Ten days' course in London; lodgings over the Poetry Bookshop

4 March Shows poems to Monro

5 March To Officers' School, Balgores House, Gidea Park

19 May On leave, first in London and then in Shrewsbury, pending gazette

4 June Commissioned into the Manchester Regiment

18 June Reports to 5th (Reserve) Battalion, Manchester Regiment, at Milford Camp, near Witley, Surrey

7 July Attached for a musketry course to 25th Battalion, Middlesex Regiment, Talavera Barracks, Aldershot

Mid-July Weekend leave at Kidmore End, near Reading, home of cousin Leslie Gunston (ELG). To church at Dunsden and sees Revd Wigan

Early August To Mytchett Musketry Camp, Farnborough, in command of the 5th Manchesters contingent

Early September Applies for transfer to Royal Flying Corps; interviewed in London, but is not transferred

14 September Visit from HO

24 September 5th Manchesters move to Oswestry, under canvas

19–20 October 5th Manchesters to Southport, Lancashire, the officers in Queen's Hotel. WO has lodgings for a few days at 168a Lord Street

c. 5 November To the firing ranges at Fleetwood in command of the battalion and brigade firing parties. Lodgings at 111 Bold Street, Fleetwood

8 December Back to Southport

Christmas Embarkation leave

29 December To France and Base Camp, Étaples

1917   *1–2 January* Joins 2nd Manchesters on the Somme near Beaumont Hamel, in a rest area. Assumes command of 3 Platoon, A Coy.

6 January 2nd Manchesters on the move towards front

9–16 January Holds dug-out in no man's land; sentry blinded

20 January Into line again; platoon exposed in severe frost

4 February Arrives at Abbeville for a course on transport duties.

25 February Leaves Abbeville

1 March Rejoins battalion near Fresnoy; posted to B Coy.

14/15 March Concussion following fall at Le Quesnoy-en-Santerre

15 March Evacuated to Military Hospital at Nesle

17 March Moved to 13th Casualty Clearing Station at Gailly

4 April Rejoins battalion at Selency.

8 April Battalion is relieved, and pulls back to Beauvois

12 April Into the line again at Savy Wood for 12 days

21 April 14th Brigade relieved; into cellar quarters at Quivières

2 May Evacuated to 13th CCS with shell-shock

11 June To No. 1 General Hospital, Etretat

16 June To Welsh Hospital, Netley, Hampshire

26 June Arrives at Craiglockhart War Hospital, Slateford, near Edinburgh

Early July Visited by Susan Owen

17 July Writes first contribution to *The Hydra*; becomes editor

Late July Siegfried Sassoon (SS) arrives at Craiglockhart

30 July Talks to 'Field Club' on 'Do Plants Think?'

c. 17 August Introduces himself to SS

1 September 'Song of Songs' published in *The Hydra*

25 September Gives first of several lessons in English literature

at Tynecastle School, Edinburgh; appears before Medical
Board

13 October Introduced by SS to Robert Graves, who is
shown draft of 'Disabled'

28 October Appears before Medical Board; three weeks' leave
pending return to unit

3 November To London

4 November To Shrewsbury

9 November Lunches and dines with Robert Ross at the
Reform Club and meets Arnold Bennett and H. G. Wells

10 November Dines again with Ross, Wells, and Bennett and
meets A. G. Gardiner, editor of the *Daily News*

11 November Visits ELG near Winchester

14 November Sees Monro at the Poetry Bookshop

24 November Joins 5th Manchesters at Scarborough for light
duties; appointed 'major-domo' of the Officers' Mess,
Clarence Gardens Hotel

4 December Promoted Lieutenant

19–23 December Short leave; to Edinburgh, revisiting
Craiglockhart and Tynecastle School

Christmas SS posted back to France

1918 *23 January* Attends Graves's marriage to Nancy Nicholson at
St James's Piccadilly. Meets Charles Scott Moncrieff

26 January 'Miners' published in *The Nation*

12 March To Northern Command Depot, Ripon

c. 23 March Into lodgings at 7 Borrage Lane, Ripon

9–11 April Weekend leave in Shrewsbury and last meeting
with HO

22 April Upgraded to Division 4

10 May Upgraded to Division 3

Mid-May 'Song of Songs' published in *The Bookman*

16–19 May In London, staying in flat over Ross's in Half
Moon Street. Visits War Office; meets Osbert Sitwell at
Ross's flat

21 May Upgraded to Division 2

4 June Graded fit for general service

5 June Rejoins 5th Manchesters at Scarborough

11 June Request from Edith and Osbert Sitwell for poems to
include in *Wheels 1918*

15 June 'Hospital Barge' and 'Futility' published in *The Nation*

Mid-June CO joins the R.A.F.

13 July SS wounded and invalided home

Mid-July HO sails to join the light cruiser *Astraea* at Simonstown

12–18 August Embarkation leave; sees SS in hospital in London; spends evening with SS and Osbert Sitwell

31 August Reports again to Base Camp, Étaples

9 September To Reception Depot, Amiens, to await arrival of 2nd Manchesters

15 September 2nd Manchesters arrive at Amiens

29 September–3 October Successful assault on Beaurevoir-Fonsomme line. Awarded M.C.

5 October Battalion back to rest area at Hancourt. Robert Ross dies in London

29 October At St. Souplet, into line for the last time

30–31 October Battalion takes over the line west of the Oise-Sambre Canal, near Ors, in preparation for an attack across the canal at dawn on 4 November

4 November Killed in early morning on the canal bank

11 November News of WO's death reaches Shrewsbury. Armistice signed

INTRODUCTION

The poems of Wilfred Owen present an editor with uncommon problems
that call for uncommon solutions. He lived to see only five in print: 'Song
of Songs' in *The Hydra* and *The Bookman*; 'The Next War' in *The Hydra*;
'Miners', 'Futility', and 'Hospital Barge' in *The Nation*. Six months before
his death, he told his mother: 'I am to have my work typed at once, and
send it to Heinemann, who is certain to send it to [Robert] Ross to read
for him!!'[1] No such typescript has ever come to light, but it is hard to
believe that any poet capable of writing 'Exposure', 'Strange Meeting', or
'Spring Offensive' would be content to leave such poems in the form in
which they have passed to posterity – manuscripts much corrected and,
in many cases, clearly unfinished. In the absence of a final typescript,
however, an editor must do what he can with what he has.

Siegfried Sassoon and Edith Sitwell were the first to thread their way
through the maze of manuscripts. Sassoon's 1920 edition of Owen's *Poems*
contained 23 poems and fragments, and a 24th was added for the 1921
reissue. Edmund Blunden's 1931 edition added 35 more, though 2 were
halves of the same poem, and his notes quoted another 2 in full. In 1963, C.
Day Lewis penetrated deeper into the maze for his edition of *The Collected
Poems*, and published a further 19 for the first time. In his Introduction he
wrote: 'In general, my text will not often be found to differ greatly from
Blunden's.' But over the years the need for a radical review of the text
became increasingly clear to scholars and critics, among them Dr Dominic
Hibberd, whose 1973 selection, *Wilfred Owen / War Poems and Others*,
departed from Day Lewis's text (of the 55 poems the two had in common)
at more than 60 points. Hibberd wished to depart more radically still, but
was discouraged by the copyright holders and publishers, on the grounds
that an edition of the *Complete Poems and Fragments* was already in
preparation.

The major problem confronting Owen's editors has not been the
legibility of his manuscripts – though some are difficult, some impossible
to read – but their chronology. In deciding the sequence of drafts and
choosing those that show the poet's latest revisions, my distinguished
predecessors had to rely almost exclusively on internal evidence. I have
been more fortunate, first, in having the benefit of their skilled reading of
such evidence; secondly, in having access not only to all the verse
manuscripts, which are mainly undated, but to all of Owen's letters, which

---

1 *Wilfred Owen/Collected Letters*, edited by Harold Owen and John Bell (1967), 552.

are mainly dated.[2] This has made possible an analysis of their paper, which has shed light on many of the darker places of the maze. Scrutiny of the verse manuscripts revealed 22 different watermarks (2 of them in paper with both a larger and a smaller size), 16 of which are to be found in dated letters. The manuscripts and letters also have in common several varieties of paper lacking a watermark, but distinct in size, colour, and texture; though there are occasional variations in size between sheets from the same 'batch' of paper, either because the manufacturer did not precisely align the sheets before guillotining (some are not cut square), or because the poet halved or otherwise cropped his page. Appendix C of *The Complete Poems and Fragments* (hereinafter CP&F) sets out in its table of paper sizes and watermarks much, but by no means all, of the evidence for dating the manuscripts. Other clues are to be found in letters, and in the matching of ink, pencil, and handwriting. There is, for example, the case of Owen's capital I's. These tend to be curved like a closing bracket J until, in August 1914, he switches to J, which he employs until May 1915 when he changes to the simpler I. All such evidence must, of course, be used with caution. There is a great deal of it, however, and most of it is both mutually supportive and supported by – or not at variance with – internal evidence yielded by the text.

The result of all this is a much more complicated chronology. Where editors and critics have tended to speak of individual poems as 'early' or 'late', many can now be seen to have been written over a considerable period; like 'Exposure', begun in December 1917, revised in early 1918, and further revised that September. The case of 'Exposure' is the more cautionary in that one of its manuscripts appears to be dated 'Feb. 1916'. Other of Owen's own dates on his manuscripts turn out to be misleading, particularly dates in titles such as 'From My Diary, 1914'. The discovery – on unarguable watermark evidence – that this poem was written in 1917/18, rather than 1914, radically alters the received view of Owen's development of pararhyme.[3]

With the dating of individual manuscripts, there became apparent the need not only for a thorough overhaul of the texts of poems previously

2 There are major collections of the verse manuscripts in the Manuscript Students' Room of the British Library in London and the English Faculty Library at Oxford. A few other manuscripts, detailed in the text, are in private hands. Most of the letters are held in the Humanities Research Center of the University of Texas. Those to Leslie Gunston were presented by him to the English Faculty Library at Oxford; seven to Siegfried Sassoon are in the Columbia University Library; and a few to the other recipients are in private hands.
3 See, for example, Dennis Welland, *Wilfred Owen / A Critical Study* (1960; revised and enlarged, 1978), 112–13.

published, but for further exploration and exposition of the intricate 'root system' underlying the published and the unpublished. Critics have noted the connections between the fragments, 'All Sounds have been as Music' and 'Bugles Sang',[4] and 'Anthem for Doomed Youth', and a number of similar connections appear in the pages of CP&F. Many fragments, of course, have no such connections – or none that I have detected – and some have little or no literary merit. Why then was it decided to print them? To present for the first time a map of Owen's poetic development, that edition offered in one chronological sequence the latest text of every poem and fragment. The poems appeared first; an account of their manuscripts, second; and the fragments third. To those readers who ask whether Owen would have wanted it this way, one can only reply that it is hard to imagine the poet who would discourage a serious interest in his poems; or who would think it logical to print all his letters and fragments of letters but not all his poems and fragments of poems.

The present edition, which can be read in conjunction with the second volume of CP&F by anyone wishing to have text, notes, and manuscript material before them at the same time, is organized as follows:

THE POEMS (pp. 1–171)

Printed here are all but seven of the poems published in CP&F; the omissions being minor pieces of juvenilia (CP&F, 8, 16, 17, 27, 29, 61, and 64). The poems in both editions are ordered by date of final revision rather than first composition. Since the text in each case reflects the poet's latest intentions, it would have been misleading to place the poems and fragments in a chronology determined by his earliest intentions. The successive stages of composition are detailed and dated in the notes following each poem. Problems remain, of course, such as the dates of composition of the sonnets (pp. 80–96) revised and fair-copied, probably for Sassoon at Craiglockhart in October–November 1917, or conceivably at Scarborough between November 1917 and January 1918. 'The Unreturning' is known to have been begun in 1912/13, 'The Sleeping Beauty' in 1914, and others may be as early or earlier. Following an account of the date, place, and circumstances of composition, the notes on each poem offer any information relevant to its biographical, historical, and literary context.

To avoid excessive repetition of material, I give frequent page references

4 In both editions, where untitled fragments are titled by the first line of the manuscript, these appear respectively as 'I know the music' (p. 178) and 'But I was looking at the permanent stars' (p. 179).

to my biography, *Wilfred Owen* (1974), in the notes. Those references printed in bold face are to photo-facsimiles of manuscripts reproduced in the biography. Some dates assigned to poems and fragments in this edition differ from those given in the biography, and should be understood to supersede them.

By the standard that defines an unfinished poem as a fragment, many of Owen's would be classed as fragmentary. If some of the decisions I have made in this respect appear arbitrary, supporting facts will be found in or accompanying the transcripts of the manuscripts.

THE MANUSCRIPTS OF THE POEMS (CP&F, pp. 195–379)

The notes to each poem make reference to the relevant page of CP&F on which the manuscript or manuscripts are described and in some cases transcribed. The sequence of manuscripts (and, on occasion, type-scripts) is set out chronologically; the last listed being the copy-text unless stated to the contrary.

In the case of pre-1914 poems, an apparatus criticus lists any signifi-cant substantive variants from the copy-text. Spelling and punctuation have been silently emended.

In the case of 1914–18 poems, all variants from the copy-text are recorded except when a full transcript of the manuscript is given. Where manuscripts other than copy-text – of poems either early or late – shed light on the genesis of the work, transcripts of these in chronological sequence (earliest first) follow a line of five spaced dots dividing such subsidiary material from the treatment of the copy-text.

THE FRAGMENTS (pp. 173–92)

CP&F prints the latest version of each fragmentary poem with notes comparable to those on the completed poems. Where an earlier version or versions illuminate/s this or another poem/fragment, it or they follow a line of five spaced dots. Eleven of these fragments, together with Owen's draft Preface, have been selected for inclusion in the present edition and their texts heavily edited for the benefit of the general reader.

While it is unlikely that any more poems by Wilfred Owen will come to light, some fragments may. The whereabouts of certain manuscripts cited in this edition are unknown. The poet's mother and his brother Harold each, on occasion, gave manuscripts to friends.

On New Year's Eve 1917, Owen wrote: 'I go out of this year a Poet, my dear Mother, as which I did not enter it. I am held peer by the Georgians; I am a poet's poet.'[5] Subsequent years have proved him right. After the recognition of his contemporaries, Graves, Sassoon, the Sitwells, came the recognition of the poets of the Thirties, Auden, Day Lewis, and Spender. The major editions of Owen's poems have all been undertaken by poets. Whether this has been to their advantage it is not for me to say, but I like to think the young man proud to be 'a poet's poet' would have approved, and would perhaps have been tolerant of the errors inevitable in the fulfilment of a task involving many thousands of decisions.

5 *Collected Letters*, 521.

LIST OF ABBREVIATIONS

WO	Wilfred Owen	HO	Harold Owen (brother)
CDL	C. Day Lewis	MO	Mary Owen (sister)
CO	Colin Owen (brother)	OS	Osbert Sitwell
DH	Dominic Hibberd	SO	Susan Owen (mother)
EB	Edmund Blunden	SS	Siegfried Sassoon
ELG	Leslie Gunston		

PRINCIPAL PUBLISHED SOURCES

By Wilfred Owen:

CDL *The Collected Poems of Wilfred Owen*, edited with an Introduction and Notes by C. Day Lewis (London, 1963)

CL *Wilfred Owen / Collected Letters*, edited by Harold Owen and John Bell (London, 1967)

CP&F *Wilfred Owen/The Complete Poems and Fragments*, edited by Jon Stallworthy (London, 1983)

DH *Wilfred Owen / War Poems and Others*, edited with an Introduction and Notes by Dominic Hibberd (London, 1973)

EB *The Poems of Wilfred Owen*, edited with a Memoir by Edmund Blunden (London, 1931)

SS Wilfred Owen, *Poems*, with an Introduction by Siegfried Sassoon (London, 1920)

OTHER SOURCES

Bäckman Sven Bäckman, *Tradition Transformed / Studies in the Poetry of Wilfred Owen* (Lund, Sweden, 1979)

JFO Harold Owen, *Journey from Obscurity*, 3 vols. (London, 1963–5)

N&Q *Notes and Queries*

RES *Review of English Studies*

Welland Dennis Welland, *Wilfred Owen / A Critical Study*, revised and enlarged edition (London, 1978)

WO Jon Stallworthy, *Wilfred Owen* (London, 1974)

All other sources are given in full in the text.

THE POEMS

TO POESY

A thousand suppliants stand around thy throne,
Stricken with love for thee, O Poesy.
I stand among them, and with them I groan,
And stretch my arms for help. Oh, pity me!
5   No man (save them thou gav'st the right to ascend
And sit with thee, 'nointing with unction fine,
Calling thyself their servant and their friend)
Has loved thee with a purer love than mine.
For, as thou yieldest thy fair self so free
10 To Masters not a few, so wayward men
Give half their adoration up to thee,
Beseech another goddess guide their pen,
And with another muse their pleasure take.
Not so with me! I neither cease to love,
15 Nor am content to love but for the sake
Of passing pleasures caught from thee above.
For some will listen to thy trembling voice
Since in its mournful music warbling low,
Or in its measured chants, or bubbling joys
20 They hear belovèd tunes of long ago.
And some are but enamoured of thy grace
And find it well to kneel to thee, and pray,
Because there oft-times play upon thy face
Smiles of an earthly maiden far away.

25 Before the eyes of all thou hast the power
To spread Elysium. Gorgeous memories
Of days far distant in the past can flower
Afresh beneath thy touch; yet not for these
Thy mighty spells I love and hymn thy name;
30 Nor yet because thou know'st the unseen road
Which leads unto the awful halls of Fame,
Where, midst the heapèd honours, thine the load
Most richly prized, of all the crowns the best!
No! not for these I long to win thee, Sweet!
35 No more is this my fervent, hopeless quest –
To stand among the great ones there, to meet
The bards of old and greet them as my peers.

O impious thought! O I am mad to ask
E'en that their voice may ever reach my ears.

40   Yet show thou me the task,
That shall, as years advance, give power and skill,
Firm hands; an eye which takes all beauty in,
That I may woo thee thus, if thus thy will.
Ah, gladly would I on such task begin
45 But that I know this learning must be bought
With gold as well as toil, and gold I lack.
What then? Dost bid me first seek out the Court
Where this world's wretched god, the money-sack,
Doles out his favours to the cringing herd,
50 There slave for him awhile to earn his pelf?

E'en should I leave him soon, my heart is stirred
With glorious fear and trembles in itself,
When I look forth upon the vasty seas
Of learning to be travelled o'er.
                              I fain
55 Would know the hills, the founts, the very trees,
Where sang the Greeks of old. I would have plain
Before my vision, heroes, poets, kings,
Hear their clear accents; then observe where trod
E'en mythic men; yea, next on Hermes' wings
60 Would mount Olympus and discern each god.

All this to speed my suit with Poesy
Meseems must do; and far, far more than this;
In divers tongues my thoughts must flow out free;
And, in my own tongue, with no word amiss,
65 For all its writers must be known to me.
My hand must wield the critic's weapons, too,
To save myself, or strike an enemy.
Oh grant that this long training ne'er undo
My simple, ardent love! Throw early dews
70 Of inspiration oft-times on my brow.
Let them fall suddenly and darkly as thou choose,
Uncertain, fitful as the thunder-drops
Which sprinkle us then cease, to splash once more

Rapidly round, still pausing for long stops,
75 Not knowing if to vent their heavy store
Upon the parching ground, or wait awhile
Till hasty travelling winds bring increased worth.
But as at last the concentrated pile
Of seething vapours flings its might to earth
80 In spurts of fire and rain, and to the ground
Flashes its energy, yields up its very soul,
So, midst long triumph-roars of awful sound,
Flash thou thy soul to me at last, and roll
Torrential streams of thought upon my brain,
85 So give, yea give Thyself to me
At last.
We shall be happy, thou and I. In me
Thou'lt find a jealous guardian of thy charms,
A doting master, leaving all to be
90 Ever with thee, ever in thine arms.
Forget my youth, forget my ignorance,
Spurn not my lowliness, and lack of friends
Who might help on my progress and perchance
Present me fearless at the throne where bends
95 Full timidly my lonely being now.
Friends' service would be naught if thine own hand
Uplifted me; do not thine eyes endow
Far brighter wealth than books, and far more grand?
Then come! Come with a rushing impulse swift,
100 Or draw near slowly, gently, so it be
Never to part.
                    Round us the world may drift,
Some with scoffs and frowns, with laughter some:
Their hateful mockery I shall not heed.
How could I feel ashamed to stand with one
105 Who deigns to stoop and be my life's high meed?
Yet if I would not for its jeering shun
The world, no more would I parade its courts
To change those jeers to applause by showing men
Thy power. Publicity but poorly sorts
110 My sacred joy, if thou should'st guide my pen.

Loath would I be to show my exceeding bliss

Even to closest friends. But all unseen,
And far from men's gaze would I feel thy kiss;
No witness save the speechless star-lamps keen
115 When thou stoop'st over me. No eye
But Cynthia's look on us, when through the night
We sit alone, our faces pressing nigh,
Quietly shining in her quiet light.

Written probably in 1909–10, this supplication to the muse owes much to
Keats's 'The Fall of Hyperion' (WO, 53–4).

TITLE Cp. Tennyson, 'To Poesy'.
    52 glorious fear: Cp. 'O World of many worlds, O life of lives' (p. 48),
        l. 33: 'O glorious fear!'
116–18 Cp. Coleridge, 'Frost at Midnight', l. 74: 'Quietly shining to the quiet
        Moon'.

CP&F, 197

[6]

WRITTEN IN A WOOD, SEPTEMBER 1910

Full ninety autumns hath this ancient beech
Helped with its myriad leafy tongues to swell
The dirges of the deep-toned western gale,
And ninety times hath all its power of speech
5 Been stricken dumb, at sound of winter's yell,
Since Adonais, no more strong and hale,
Might have rejoiced to linger here and teach
His thoughts in sonnets to the listening dell;
Or glide in fancy through those leafy grots
10 And bird-pavilions hung with arras green,
To hear the sonnets of its minstrel choir.
Ah, ninety times again, when autumn rots
Shall birds and leaves be mute and all unseen,
Yet shall I see fair Keats, and hear his lyre.

Written – as indicated by its title – in September 1910, this sonnet testifies to
WO's early admiration for the poems of Keats and Shelley (WO, 53).

  1 Full ninety autumns: Keats died in Rome on 21 February 1821.
  6 Adonais: Shelley's name for Keats in his pastoral elegy with that title.
  9 those leafy grots: Cp. Keats, *Endymion*, ii. 921: 'the lofty grot'.

CP&F, 197

SONNET
Written at Teignmouth, on a Pilgrimage to Keats's House

Three colours have I known the Deep to wear;
'Tis well today that Purple grandeurs gloom,
Veiling the Emerald sheen and Sky-blue glare.
Well, too, that lowly-brooding clouds now loom
5 In sable majesty around, fringed fair
With ermine-white of surf: to me they bear
Watery memorials of His mystic doom
Whose Name was writ in Water (saith his tomb).

Eternally may sad waves wail his death,
10 Choke in their grief 'mongst rocks where he has lain,
Or heave in silence, yearning with hushed breath,
While mournfully trail the slow-moved mists and rain,
And softly the small drops slide from weeping trees,
Quivering in anguish to the sobbing breeze.

Begun on 21 April 1911 at Teignmouth – where Keats had lived from March to
May 1818 at 20 Northumberland Place (formerly 20 the Strand) – this sonnet
was finished at Shrewsbury shortly afterwards (WO, 57–8).

> 8 On Keats's instructions, his tombstone in Rome bears the words: 'Here
> lies one whose name was writ in water.'

CP&F, 198

[8]

LINES WRITTEN ON MY NINETEENTH BIRTHDAY
March 18, 1912

Two Spirits woke me from my sleep this morn;
Both most unwelcome were; for they have torn
Away from me the shady screens of ease
And unreflecting, unself-scanning Peace
5   Wherein I used to hide me from annoy
In years which found and left me still a Boy.
The First rose solemn, with a Voice of stern
Monition; and it said: 'Look back! and learn
To number life by moments, not by years;
10   Know that thy youth to its completion nears.
This night the final minute hath been laid
Upon thy nineteen Springs. Aye, be dismayed
To see the Fourth Part of thy utmost Span
Now spent! What then? Affrighted dost thou plan
15   To crowd the Rest with Action, every whit?
Ev'n so essay; but know thou canst not knit
Thy web of hours so close as to regain
E'en one lost stitch! For ever gaps remain!'
Hereat it ceased; for now a second Shade
20   Caught all my senses to't; no sound it made;
No form it had; but quietly it drew
Its tightening hand of Pain through every thew
Of my frail body. . . . Pain? – Why Pain today?
Sure, not a taste of what this tingling clay
25   Shall suffer through the year? And yet, if so,
'Twill be but my most rightful share, I trow,
Scarce worse than the keen hunger-pinch that racks
Numberless wretches all their life. Pain slacks
Its hold on one, only to grasp another;
30   And why should I be spared, and not my brother?

So thinking, quickly I pass the day. And lo!
What kindnesses the Friends around me show!
How many eyes in warm solicitude
Have smiled upon me! Tongues that have been rude
35   Are gentle now. . . . Yet still, how do I miss
Thine eyes, *thy* voice, my Mother! Oft I kiss

Thy portrait, and I clutch thy letter dear
As if it were thy hand.
                              At this, fresh cheer
Comes over me; and now upon my couch
40 Of ruby velvet, o'er the fire I crouch
In full content. I only pause from reading
To scribble these few lines; or, scarcely heeding
The dismal damp abroad, to mock the rain
Shooting its sleety balls at me in vain.
45 – Ho, thus, methinks, hereafter, when the weak
Creations of a Mental Mist shall seek
To quench my soul, I'll thwart them by the shield
Of crystal Hope!
                              For there have been revealed
Heart-secrets since the coming of this day,
50 Making me thankful for its thorn-paved way.
Among them this: 'No joy is comparable
Unto the *Melting* – soft and gradual –
Of Torture's needles in the flesh. To sail
Smoothly from out the abysmal anguish-jail
55 And tread the placid plains of *normal ease*
Is sweeter far, I deem, than all the glees
Which we may catch by mounting higher still
Into the dangerous air where actual Bliss doth thrill.'

Written at Dunsden on 18 March 1912 (WO, 71), these lines accompanied WO's
letter of 19 March to SO: 'But on my birthday morning I was awakened by the
unrelenting gnawings [of indigestion] within, and took a bit of toast for
breakfast. The couch from the passage was then brought down for me, and
thereon I lay all day; finding relief however very soon after breakfast-time. To
ease me, I employed my time upon the "lines", which you have, with the ink, as
it were, still wet upon them. . . . Don't be content with a first reading but if you
fail to see any point at all, 'tis no fault of yours. Consider how quickly I wrote!'
(CL, 125)

36–7 Cp. Cowper, 'On the Receipt of my Mother's Picture out of Norfolk', ll.
        1–4:
            Oh that those lips had language! Life has pass'd
            With me but roughly since I heard thee last.
            Those lips are thine – thy own sweet smiles I see,
            The same that oft in childhood solaced me . . .

CP&F, 199

[10]

SUPPOSED CONFESSIONS
OF A SECONDRATE SENSITIVE MIND
IN DEJECTION

Time was when I have loved the bards whose strains
Saddened the heart, and wrought a heavy mood;
Aye, and my spirit felt a joy to brood
O'er melodies which told of ancient pains.

5   Lovely the tones when poet's lips have moved
For very mournfulness. . . . O fair the sight
(As now we see it) of a Spirit bright
Bowed on a southern strand; his work approved
Of none; his name despised or else unknown.
10   O then, how firm and close was his embrace
Unto Despondency! – Her shadowed face,
Methought, how fair! What music in her moan!
Ye, too, have sometimes wished her near;
Loved a chill dampness round thy path, and known
15   Her voice, which like a weary wind and lone,
Fled through the woods with lamentation drear.
But think not, if your life-blood still is warm,
That ye have looked upon Despondency.
Ye have but seen her in another's eye,
20   As Perseus fearfully beheld the form
Of Gorgon, mirrored in the stilly well.
There may ye guess the beauty of that Head,
The pallor and the mystery – but the Dread
Ye feel not, nor the horror, nor the spell.

25   But, face to face, she fixed on me her stare:
Woe, woe, my blood has never moved since then;
Down-dragged like corpse in sucking, slimy fen,
I sank to feel the breath of that Despair.

With Autumn mists, and hand in hand with Night,
30   She came to me. But at the break of day,
Went not again, but stayed, and yet doth stay.
' – O Horror, doth not Pain take note of light
And darkness, – doth he not hold off betimes,
And yield his victim for an hour to Sleep?

35 Then why dost thou, O Curst, the long night steep
   In bloodiness and stains of shadowy crimes?'
   She hears my cry, and mutters yet, .
   'No rest, no rest for thee, O Slave of mine';
   Till I do hate myself and would resign
40 My life to pay a murderer's awful debt.

   Out, out to moorlands, from such thoughts I flee
   And seek the balm that fair fresh woods distil.
   There find I all things in a hushèd thrill
   For dread of that grey fiend that walks with me.

45 She leads me forth, and poisons autumn eves
   With hellish scenes; shows me an aged tree
   Bending and groaning in its agony
   Before a wind tormenting it for leaves;
   Spreads out a wild strange sky where towering shapes,
50 Black and chaotic, choke the sickening day.
   Voices moan round; and from the sodden clay
   Mist-shrouds crawl up, in token that there gapes
   A grave for me at hand.
                              Aching with fears,
   I stumble towards the town, whose distant lights
55 Glint feebly and go out, and glint again,
   Like some retreating ship's unto the ken
   Of a lost man, who, sinking, feebly fights
   Alone in the wide waste behind.
                              The murmuring tone
   Of busy streets a moment gladdens me;
60 But there, too, comes the Spirit secretly;
   At feasts I see her shade, and am alone
   With thoughts of pain and nothing hear but her.

   So that I may not handle a keen knife,
   But flashes to the mind a fearful use
65 That men have made of it, to loose
   The heavy-weighted burden of their life
   And make an end. But Death is not the end:
   No death for such as thou, O Chatterton!
   Until the Second Death; and I do shun

70 The thought that death is misery's friend.
Since my dread Ghost has once a finger laid
Upon my flesh, and left a burning mark;
This mark (saith she) shall fester on, and cark
Till Death draw near, and halting, shade
75 His withering eyes, and know the Sign.
                                        O dense
The darkness that shall flood around me then;
Denser the clouds of biting arrows, when
Vile devil-broods to torments bear me hence!

Written between September 1911 and May 1912.

TITLE Cp. Tennyson, 'Supposed Confessions of a Second-Rate Sensitive
       Mind', and Coleridge, 'Dejection: An Ode'.

  8   southern strand: WO is referring to Keats's arrival in Italy in 1820.

 20   Perseus: The son of Danaë and Zeus, in Greek mythology. Polydectes,
       king of Seriphos, wishing to get rid of Perseus, sent him to fetch the head
       of the Medusa, one of the three Gorgons whose eyes turned men to
       stone. But Pluto lent Perseus a helmet that would make him invisible,
       Athene a shield (in which to see the Gorgons' reflection), and Hermes
       wings for his feet. He was thus able to escape the Gorgons' eyes and cut
       off the Medusa's head. WO returned to this theme in a later fragment,
       'Perseus' (CP&F, 464).

63-7   Cp. Hamlet, III. i. 74-5: 'he himself might his quietus make / With a bare
       bodkin.'

67-8   Cp. Keats, 'To Chatterton', ll. 7-10:
                               Thou didst die
          A half-blown flow'ret which cold blasts amate.
          But this is past: thou art among the stars
          Of highest Heaven . . .

CP&F, 200

[13]

THE DREAD OF FALLING INTO NAUGHT

Now slows the beat of Summer's dancing pulse;
Her voice has weak and quaverous undertones;
Cold agues in her hectic limbs convulse;
Slow palsies creep into her sapless bones.
5 Ah! is she falling into Death so soon, so soon?

Ev'n so! and now the peerless forest green
Is streaked with silvery pallor of decay.
As a beauteous woman's locks may lose their sheen
Through fearful dreams, and turn too early grey,
10 So Summer paleth now, and moaneth in her swoon.

The expressions of her once-rich mind, the flowers,
Are feeble-born, else rank unnaturally;
And whoso looks on leafy garden bowers,
Fresh bloodstains every misty morn may see,
15 Spilt from her veins by Winter's lance, and conflict-strewn.

My power of life, though youthful, also sinks;
Before my time I bear a hoary head;
And chill airs strike my brow, that blow, methinks,
Straight from the icy cavern of the dead.
20 Night darkens round; my day shall know no afternoon.

O never mourn, my brothers! well ye know
These crimson stains shall vanish from the trees;
Washed by the precious ointment of the snow.
A little while, and drowsy Earth's disease,
25 Shall feel the healing quickness of another June.

I, only, mourn, because I cannot tell
What spring-renewing wakes the sleep of Men.
I do but know, (ah! this I know too well)
I shall not see the same sweet life again,
30 Nor the dear Sun, nor stars, nor tender moon.

Written at Dunsden on 18 September 1912, according to the dated MS.
17 hoary head: Cp. Keats, *Endymion*, III. 218: 'The old man rais'd his hoary head.'
CP&F, 204

[SCIENCE HAS LOOKED]

Science has looked, and sees no life but this:
Or, at the most 'tis hypothetical.
'Thou art as animals, as worms, as clay;
Earth – thy small planet, of a thousand, one –
5   Shall slowly waste, unto an outburnt ash:
And thou and all thy race, be blotted out.
For in the dissolution of man's brain
Himself dissolves, and passes into naught' . . .

O careful Science, thou had'st all my zeal,
10 But a Third Power smiles, and beckons me.
She is a wanton of too light a name
To hold the faith of most men in her heart.
Poor Poesy! She hath no constancy . . .

But yesterday she clung half-trustingly
15 To calm religion. Where is she today?
Clasping Cold Science with a grim embrace!
No constancy! But comforts manifold,
And therefore, lovely to a waif, like me!

Speak to me, Poesy! Give me on this height
20 The one true message of thy thousand oracles!

'Yea? cryest thou so hungry for some Light?
Seek light no more! There is no Light as yet!
The Light that lights the soul shall be the last
Created thing; as that which lights the eye the first!
25 These mountains are the breasts of Mother Earth,
Nestle thou there, child; suck thy fill of joys.
And strive no more to look beyond thy Mother's arms.'

– So? is it so? Then I will lie and rest.
O mountains, there comes over me this hour
30 A wondrous longing for my latest sleep.
I long to drowse, and fall upon eternal sleep;
I want to sleep, but not to dream, and not to wake;
Pass hence, and yet behold no region more;

Fade from this company of distracted men
35 Where all are mad deluders, or else sick deluded . . .

Now, Night, rise softly like a careful nurse:
Lower the lights of day round thy sick child:
For I would sleep . . .
Poor I, who know not what I am, nor whence,
40 Would shake away this bitter case of flesh,
Even though naught remain when it is gone.
Would rid me of long deceiving blood;
How know I but at this very hour
My thoughts most high, most melancholy-grand,
45 Be not the chance-distemper of my pulse,
The doing of some small, intestine flaw!
O death, before I pluck my brain away,
Let me but sleep . . .
                    My heart stops – it is well . . .
50 O Light, which art but darkness,
O cruel world . . . O Men . . . O my own Self . . .
Farewell!

Written at Dunsden between September and November 1912.

19–20 Cp. 'To Poesy' (p. 3), and Keats, 'The Fall of Hyperion', l. 147:
        'None can usurp this height.'

31–2 Cp. *Hamlet*, III. i. 64–5: 'To die; to sleep – /To sleep? Perchance to
        dream! Ay, there's the rub.'

40 Cp. *Hamlet*, I. ii. 129: 'O that this too too solid flesh would melt'; and
        Antony and Cleopatra, IV. xiv. 41: 'Crack thy frail case!'

48 Cp. 'Strange Meeting' (p. 125), l. 44: 'Let us sleep now. . . .'

CP&F, 204

[16]

THE LITTLE MERMAID
of Hans Christian Anderson

Part 1

1

Far out at sea, the water is as blue
As cornflowers, and as clear as crystal-core;
But so exceeding deep, no sea-bird's view
Can fathom it, nor men's ropes touch its floor.
5 Strange, snake-like trees and weeds – the same which grew
Before dry land with herbs was peopled o'er –
Still sleep in heavy peacefulness down there,
And hold their fluctuous arms towards upper air.

2

And it is there the Sea-King's nation dwells.
10 His palace, golden-bright and ruby-red,
Gleams like a crown among those velvet dells.
Pink, shimmering streams of light its windows shed,
Like waterfalls of wine; and pink-white shells,
Like Alpine snows, its lofty roof o'erspread;
15 Which close and open, close and open wide,
With every ebb and flowing of the tide.

3

Twice beauteous is the sight, for perfect pearls
Glimmer between the valvelets as they gape.
As when a butterfly shut wings unfurls,
20 And pollen-filmèd globes of dew escape,
So ope those shells, so shine those gems. The swirls
Of stirring currents stroke to smoothest shape
The sandy palace floors; or, like a breeze,
Suddenly fluster its mysterious trees.

4

25 The ancient King, of consort long bereft,
Unto his mother gave the queenly state;
And in her careful governance he left
His six fair daughters. Scarce could I relate

The beauty of those six without a theft
30 Of honey-words from some song-potentate;
And of the youngest's utter loveliness,
I rest content to wake a wistful guess.

5

Her skin is delicate and freshly clear
As petals of wild rose; and in her eyes,
35 As in the stillness of an evening mere,
All heaven's purple concentrated lies.
But lo! what marvel to mankind is here:
She has no feet, no knees! but mermaid-wise,
A fish's tail, smooth-tapering from her waist,
40 Blue-scaled, and glistering, like silver chased.

6

All day, these mermaids sported in their hall,
Feeding the fish that through the windows shot,
And training weeds to twine about the wall.
Or sometimes each would tend her garden grot,
45 Where one so ranged her plants as to recall
Blunt-snouted whales; another planned her plot
In shapes to imitate her own; and one,
The youngest, choosing red flowers, made a sun.

7

A strange and lonely child seemed this Princess.
50 Deep were the fathomings of her secret thought.
Not that she shunned a sisterly caress;
But, spoken to, faint-smiled, and answered naught.
Loved she the silent deep? Nay, less and less
She loved it! And as years new sameness brought,
55 Its silence, its low stillness, its pale gloom,
Weighed on her soul, and made sweet life a doom.

8

Her sisters joyed to find such curious things
As foundering ships let fall to their domain;
But she cared not for showered coins or rings,
60 And claimed no share of all that precious rain

Except a marble statue, – some boy-king's,
Or youthful hero's. Its cold face in vain
She gazed at, kissed, and tried with sighs to thaw,
For still the wide eyes stared, and nothing saw.

9

65 Thereby she set a weeping-willow tree
To droop and mourn. Full dolefully it clung
About the form, and moved continually,
As if it sighed; as if it sometimes wrung
Convulsive fingers in sad reverie.
70 And ever o'er the light blue sand it hung
A purple shade, which hour by hour the same,
Burnt softly on, like lambent sulphur flame.

10

Soon, for the twilight of that shadow's ring,
The girl forsook the fiery-blossomed grove
75 And golden-fruited gardens of the King;
Yet not e'en there her eyes reposed; but strove
For glimpses of the sun's far brightening.
Her ear could bear no voice, unless it wove
Tales of the upper world; its tuneful birds;
80 Sweet-odoured blooms; warm meadows; placid herds.

11

Long time before these wonders might be seen
By her, for it was now the year wherein
The eldest sister counted years fifteen.
(Now sea-folk hold it as unthinkable sin
85 For girls to wander from their sire's demesne
Until a certain year of age they win.)
Rose the first Princess to the waves at last,
And there, in wonderment, a long night passed.

12

Returned, she told her sisters all; and said
90 Naught was so fine as, from a sandy isle,
To watch a city's lights, white, green, and red,
Pricking the dark for many a twinkling mile.

She caught strange music, and, more strange, the tread
Of crowded men. Then, from some campanile,
95   Hummed the low voices of the midnight bells,
And bugles fluted in far citadels.

13

A year went; and the second happy maid
Broke the still surface of the evening sea.
The sky was peerless gold; a slow parade
100   Of violet clouds wheeled westward gorgeously.
Above her, like a white and fluttering braid,
The wild swans winged towards the sun. Then she
Swam westward too; but swift the great ball sank,
Leaving the air all colourless and dank.

14

105   The third Princess was bold: she made her way
Far up a river, passing vine-clad hills,
And wooded castles all the sunny day.
Oft-times she had to dive or take cool swills
To ease her burning skin. She fain would play
110   With bathing children; but with terror-shrills
They fled from her; and when dogs barked amain,
She too took fright, and turned to sea again.

15

The fourth remained in mid-seas; whence, said she,
A vast blue bell of glass appeared the vault.
115   Dim sails she spied; and watched the tireless glee
Of waggish dolphins turning somersault,
And whales a-snorting fountains angrily.
The fifth went up in winter, when like malt
The surge was frothing, and the drifting ice
120   Shone green as emerald thrones of Paradise.

16

She took a slippery seat on one of these,
And let the winds fan out her long, wet hair.
The near ships scudded on before the breeze
As if alarmed to see her. . . . Then the air

125　Fell vaporous-heavy; ocean, ill at ease,
　　　Belched spray; but safe upon her swinging chair,
　　　She laughed to see the vessels roll and leap,
　　　And lightnings zigzag o'er the seething deep.

　　　17
　　　It often happened that the sisters five
130　Would rise with arms entwined at twilight brown.
　　　O! it was sweet to see them upward drive
　　　Light as the clustered balls of thistledown.
　　　Then would they sing, and singing sometimes strive
　　　To tell storm-tossers not to fear to drown.
135　But men, who take their voices for the wind,
　　　Must perish ere they reach the sea-folk kind.

　　　18
　　　Said I those linkèd evening flights were sweet?
　　　Ah! not so unto one! . . . who stood and gazed
　　　Until the lightnings from the distant beat
140　Of lashing tails she saw no more; then raised
　　　Her eyes to where the large, pale stars did fleet
　　　Through gliding shadows, and so dreamed amazed
　　　Of shadowy ships; which guessed not the appeal
　　　Of mermaid arms outstretched towards their keel.

　　　Part II

　　　19
145　So dreamed she through the years; until, oh joy!
　　　The day of her ascension surely came.
　　　Now must the grandame tedious skill employ,
　　　In dressing her as should befit her name.
　　　Though truly all this pomp did but annoy
150　The Princess: often, with a hurt exclaim,
　　　She would have shaken off the eight large shells
　　　That decked her tail; and ev'n her asphodels.

　　　20
　　　But 'Pride must suffer pain' the dame averred,
　　　And wove the heavy wreath about her brow.

155　However, all forgotten at the word
　　　'Farewell', she shot up lightsomely enow.
　　　Many a silver bubble she bestirred
　　　To quiver up as up she sped; and now,
　　　Herself a bubble, burst upon the air,
160　And lost herself within its wonders rare.

　　　21

　　　The sun that moment dipped, but fairy pink
　　　Still flushed the clouds, and long their trailing fringe
　　　Swept on, and waved above the airy brink
　　　Where day was slipping from the earth. A tinge
165　Curdled the sea, like mingling oil and ink,
　　　Or bloody lymph when witch's flames impinge.
　　　And in the midst of that wide calm, there lay
　　　A large, dark ship, still as a rock, and grey.

　　　22

　　　Only one sail was hoist, for no breeze stirred.
170　The sailors all about the rigging hung
　　　In easy pose, each like a dozing bird.
　　　Soft music breathed at times, clear voices sung;
　　　And when the shine of eve grew blurred,
　　　Hundreds of lantern fires on high were slung.
175　Sudden, the dazzle of a rocket-glance!
　　　And on the deck strikes up the merry dance.

　　　23

　　　The mermaid, close beneath, essays to peep
　　　Through the transparent cabin panes; and oft
　　　As she is lifted by the billow-leap,
180　Espies young human forms, more beauteous-soft
　　　Than she had dreamed; but oh! she holds these cheap
　　　Beside their Prince. Anon he goes aloft,
　　　Whereat a hundred fireworks skyward hiss,
　　　Fright'ning the maid far down the dark abyss.

　　　24
185　When next she looks, the stars of heaven seem falling;
　　　Suns drizzle sparks, and all is light as day.

So that amid the din and flash appalling,
She clearly sees the glistening pleasure-ray
Gleam from the Prince's eye, as he is calling
190 For songs, and smiling on his comrades gay.
Why is his smile so sparkling and elate?
Surely his birthday they must celebrate!

25

See how the poesy trembles on his lip
To hear the pining violins, heart torn,
195 Yearn to the lightsome harps, that o'er them trip,
Like elves about Titania, love-lorn!
Ah, hark, though – in the shrouds above the ship –
How envious winds now bodefully 'gin mourn!
The sighing of their wailful harmonies
200 Hath hushed the lutings and the chaunted glees.

26

It is late. Starry lamps and fierce fusees
Fade out. The stunning guns are dumb. All ears
Hark to grumbling in the heart of the seas.
The ship makes sudden headway; on she steers,
205 Her canvas spreading to the strengthening breeze;
Till lightning shows a dark shore quickly nears.
Whereat the mariners reef again the sails,
And know they lie at mercy of the gales.

27

The mermaid, clinging to the vessel's side,
210 Bounding from crest to crest with dizzy swoop,
Fancies they run a right good billow-ride.
The crew, all huddled on the drenching poop,
Think differently. Fresh leaks split gaping-wide;
A mountain-wave bursts o'er a shrieking group,
215 And sweeps them deep into the deep cold.
The mast falls headlong; water fills the hold;

28

She heels slowly – leans – sinks – O Heaven – she sinks!
With gasp and bubbling groan the brave ship goes,
She and her braver souls. . . . The nymph but thinks
220   Of one; and him, just as his eyelids close,
Just as his mouth draws in the first death-drinks,
She finds, upholds, and guides between the floes
Of battling planks and spars of splintering wood.
Then lets the billows bear them where they should.

29

225   At dawn, the outspent wind sank down as dead;
And gloriously uprist the eastern hues.
They touched the Prince's pallid cheek with red,
And soon with certain life he did infuse.
The nereid kissed him; fondled his fine head,
230   And smoothed his hair so marred with clammy ooze.
He seemed her statue grown life-sensitive!
She kissed again, and knew that he would live.

30

Now they approached a balmy, sunlit land,
Whose marble mountains, silver-tipped with snow,
235   Towered o'er a seaboard fringe of citrons bland.
She swam to where a domèd portico
Crowned shallow waves; and, passing up the sand,
Laid down her sleeping burden there-below.
Then she drew back, and hid beneath thick foam,
240   To watch for whoso thitherward might roam.

31

Ere long there issued from that building white,
A crowd of straying girls. Soon one of these
Beheld the prostrate corse; half choked with fright,
She uttered cries; then, falling on her knees,
245   Besought him speak. He stared, smiled, rose upright.
And with those maidens vanished through the trees.
But no smile sent he to the watching one,
Nor knew he aught of all that she had done.

32

Stricken, as with a wound, she stiffly fell
250 Into her father's halls; and from that hour,
Her pensiveness increased tenfold. 'What spell',
They asked her, 'doth thy budding life deflower?
Show us this hidden woe. Thou wilt not tell?
Sister, what sights of ship, or cloud or tower,
255 Bewitched thee on thy happy day above?'
– Empty request! How dared she say 'twas Love!

33

Till, after lingering by that quiet beach,
Marking the dazzling snow-caps slowly melt,
Fruits ripen, cornfields mellow, pastures bleach,
260 And last, the acorn showers begin to pelt,
But seeing nevermore the Prince, her speech
Could hold no more: all, all she felt
And longed for, poured she out in piteous sobs.
And lo! in flooded Hope with glorious throbs!

34

265 For none among her kindred maids but burned
To help their sister's love, so destitute;
And 'twas not long ere one of them had learned
Where dwelt this Prince of high terrene repute.
So henceforth her fond spirit no more yearned
270 Unto a vision, once-seen, stark and mute,
But now she held him in her constant sight,
And stayed beneath his casement night by night.

35

He thought himself alone on many a night
While she was close; and gave no noteful heed,
275 When, in the shadows, murmured ripples slight.
Once, ev'n, as she was hid in bedded reed,
A gust seized hold her silvery veil so light.
But he who saw, must needs the rest instead,
By saying: 'Lo! a swan that spreads its wings!'
280 – How blind are men to twilight's mystic things!

Part III

36

Much looking and much brooding on the earth,
Desire unsated, daily growing worse,
Begot in her young brain the sudden birth
Of an idea – too strange for her to nurse.
285 Therefore with fervidness, though feigning mirth,
She brought it to the Queen: 'Sweet dame, rehearse
More and yet more of the world that's dry.
Bears it immortal lives? Or do men die?'

37

So she began, and thus the Queen replied:
290 'They die, my child, they die. And their life's term
Is shorter than our own. We here abide
Three hundred years; then, like the basest worm,
Dissolve into the foamy ocean-tide.
Now men have brief existence and infirm,
295 But after, they ascend beyond the stars,
Where tears are not, and naught their rapture mars.'

38

'And why have we no such undying soul?
Oh, I would give my mermaid centuries
For one day human, and Hope's aureole.'
300 'Think not of that; we of the underseas',
The lady said, 'live happier and more whole
Than men do, with their early grave, disease,
And void despairs. For not all hope as thou,
Nor is Life's crown for every human brow.'

39

305 'So, at the last, to empty surf I melt;
Drift on the gabbling waves, yet hear no word;
Froth in the soft, warm rains, that fall unfelt;
Fly before whistling winds that pipe unheard
And know no more the place where I have dwelt.'
310 'And better so! Why, 'less reports have erred,
Many a human life hath envied thine,
And thy long sleep upon the windy brine.'

40

'But is there no way whereby I might find
A spirit like to man's?' 'No way, dear girl,
315 Unless it chanced some rashling of their kind,
So loved you that you were to him a pearl,
More goodly than his own wide world enshrined,
And wedded you. Nay, mark! 'Twould be a churl
Who'd do it. This magnificent tail of yours
320 Offends their youth. Four limbs, else no men-wooers!

41

'Come, come, be merry! Let us leap about
During the span of years we have to live.
Thou'lt find it long enough, beyond a doubt,
To welcome Death, a blessèd lenitive.
325 Tonight we give a ball: attend this rout;
'Twill stir thy wits: thou'rt too contemplative.'
In radiant revelry soon came the mermen all
And nymphs, and staring fishes, great and small.

42

For ocean hummed with music through and through
330 And the shades were phosphor-sheened. 'Rejoice! Rejoice!'
The dancers sang; the Princess chanted too,
Delighted; and that night she knew her voice
To be the loveliest and most flawless-true
E'en heard on land or sea. Yet 'twas her choice
335 To steal away from all the vast applause,
Unto her garden, there from mirth to pause.

43

A bugle sounded through the far dark wave.
'Ah, now', she moaned, 'he surely sails aloft;
He for whose warm, celestial love I crave;
340 He who could give me in two kisses soft
All joy in life, and all beyond the grave.
Lo! I will venture all for him! What oft
I feared, tonight I'll face. What other help?'
Thereat she 'gan to wind through groves of kelp,

345 Towards the abysmal deserts, where the flood
Spins fierce in spiral phantasies; which, crossed,
Led to a region of warm, bubbling mud,
With slimy weeds and greenery bemossed,
And serpent-polypi, that feed on blood,
350 And hug old rust, gaunt hulks and treasures lost.
Between their ever-groping arms the lithe girl shot,
A shuddering lightning; then sank safe – on what?

45
– The witch's den! Around was filthy quag,
In whose soft mire slow-wallowed water slugs,
355 Large, fat, and white. There sat the fishy hag,
Beneath her hut of bones. About her dugs
Clung toads; while snakes, with lazy drag,
Wound round her arms, which she, with fulsome hugs,
Embraced and stroked, and fed from her own mouth.
360 This horror parched the maid's full voice like drouth.

46
'I know, I know why thou art come, fair fool!
Would'st rid thee of thy tail, and wear instead
Two props, according to the earth-folk's rule;
All this that some young prince may love and wed
365 Thy beauty. So, too, shall ye overrule
High fate, which orders that our dead keep dead,
Not live for aye, as men do fable. Bah!
Hoo-hoo! Buy legs to steal thee wings! Ha-ha!'

47
So loud and so repulsive laughed the witch,
370 The very reptiles fell upon the ground,
And there lay wriggling. Then 'I'm not so rich',
Quoth she, 'as to refuse a Princess crowned.
Have thy mad will. I'll charm a potion which,
Mark ye! shall give thee legs, straight, white, and sound,
375 But hurt it must as swords were probing ye.
Drink it at sunrise, sitting near the sea.

48

'All who behold thee in thy changèd state
Shall call thee fairest mortal, beauty's queen.
Thine agile, floating elegance of gait
380 Thou shalt retain; no dancer ever seen
May move so light as thou. But wait, child, wait!
Each step ye take will cost ye pain as keen
As if ye trod on knives. An ye do choose
To bear these pangs, my magic I will use.'

49

385 'I do,' replied the mermaid; but she shook
As shake the weeds below the surface-storm.
'Bethink ye well: thy fish-tail once forsook,
Ye cannot change again from human form,
Nor ever on thy father's Palace look.
390 And should ye find your Prince not quite so warm,
And fail to win his love – such love that he
Break from his old delights to cleave to thee –

50

'Thou diest: the soul thou reachest after, missed;
Life thrown away. The day he weds his choice
395 Shall be thy last. Ocean shall be thy cist;
His solemn breast, spurned for a fickle boy's,
Shall nurse thee; shrivelled into spumy mist!
And now, child, pay my dues. I want thy voice.
Needest its tones to charm him, little witch?
400 Nay, give thy best for this my ichor rich.'

51

'But if thou take my voice, what have I left?'
'Thy buoyancy! Thy matchless mould! Thine eyes!
Come! Let me cut thy tongue, nor think it theft.'
'Take it! . . . O Prince! . . . O sweet immortal prize!'
405 Pale as a faint moon in a stormy cleft
Was her drawn mouth, and wild as winds her sighs.
But from complaint she utterly forbore.
So yielded up her voice, and spake no more.

52

Forthwith the sorceress brought forth her pot,
410 And having scoured it well with knotted snakes,
Dripped in from her own veins black bloody clot;
Then added poisons, bones, and weird mandrakes;
So that there roamed around the cauldron hot,
Fumes such as rise when rousèd Etna quakes.
415 Whilst the loud simmering of that mystic chyle
Droned like the wailings of a crocodile.

53

These spells complete, the mermaid took the juice,
Which seemed as water from the purest fount,
Safe passed the polyps and the whirling sluice
420 (For the dread charm o'er these was paramount).
Then, hovering o'er her home, she strove to loose
Love's hindering thongs from round her heart. But 'Mount!'
A stronger Love was crying, 'Fast to shore!'
So, in great grief, she slowly 'gan to soar.

54

425 While yet the sapphire night bedomed the world,
Aground, and 'neath the palace water stair,
Waiting the charmèd dawn, she lay upcurled.
In swoon she lay, and she was unaware
How, after break of day, the wavelets purled
430 About her feet, and licked her ankles bare.
But so it was: the potion of the seer
Had worked its work, and heaven was very near.

Part IV

55

The pang that broke her sleep was quickly spent,
Quenched in a bliss, above all blisses sweet:
435 None other than the Prince above her bent!
Their earnest eyes like magnet-steels did meet.
She, dropping lids before his gaze intent,
First saw her marble shining limbs complete;
And joyed. But on the instant was amate,
440 For from her eyes no word could he translate.

56

Much wond'ring why so rich a mouth were mute,
He gently led her towards the stately door.
Even as she foreknew, stabbings acute
Tortured her tread; which willingly she bore,
445 Although she looked to see the blood out-shoot.
But no stain lay upon the yellow shore.
Only the ribbèd sand was soft and sodden,
Molten to jelly, where her soles had trodden.

57

Thus hand in hand with him her beauteous Prince,
450 Up the broad steps she flew, like wafted bubble.
– And never was she known to cry or wince,
For all the anguish of that secret trouble.
And then they dressed her, as before or since,
Few girls have been. For favour she had double
455 The other inmates of that courtly place.
And all the land made marvel at her face.

58

The Prince soon found a name to call her by:
Philotis; which was linked on many a lip
With his name, Philo, in a tone full sly.
460 Greatly he loved to watch her deft feet trip.
For slaves would frisk, and swim, and sprawl and fly,
But tiptoe Lotis almost seemed to slip
Into the air and float upon her arms.
So more the realm was ravished by her charms.

59

465 Those slaves would also sing, with mimic glee.
Ah, why should young Philotis fall so sad,
When Philo praised them? – 'Twas not jealousy!
But soon a heavier grief than this she had:
Though loved as any fair young child might be,
470 Though dear as many a lass to one same lad,
She was not the devotion of his life;
He never dreamed to take her as his wife.

Long, long she feared to think it; yet 'twas plain;
And every day the certainty increased.
475 By night, new thoughts would steal upon her brain
Wild as the far-off cry of some strange beast.
And Philo's sweetest laugh became her bane.
And though his merry kisses had not ceased,
She knew her mouth, that never might unclose,
480 Must seem a blighted bud, a scentless rose.

61

And thus she let her colour fade away,
And languished for cool waters, like a flower.
The more so when her sisters left their play
To watch continually beneath her tower,
485 And nightly sing how sore was their dismay.
Once, she perceived the King, for one short hour,
And once the agèd Queen; but not anear.
They had not risen so for many a year.

62

'My Lotis,' said Prince Philo, one soft eve,
490 'My parents wish me married, as you know,
And bid me see their choice; but had I leave,
I would not think of this same Princess. No!
I love not an unknown. I had as lieve
Wed thee, Philotis, as commit me so.
495 For thou resemblest one I love full well,
Who saved my life: a heavenly damosel.

63

'When I was wrecked, and cast on foreign shore,
She succoured me; she saved me from the sea.
Twice saw I her; I shall not see her more.
500 But something of her beauty lives in thee.
Forgive me if too ardently I pore
Upon thy face; kind fate has sent thee me,
And thou hast driven her image from my heart.
Kiss me, Philotis; we must never part.'

64

505 So when he sailed away in gallant state,
To meet the daughter of a neighbouring king,
Lotis went with him. Then to her he'd prate
Of calms and tempests; fishes; everything
The deep reveals where divers penetrate,
510 Supposing that she listened wondering.
And sooth she gazed into the waves full hard,
As if they were not dark to her regard.

65

Both day and night her lonely watch she kept,
Leaning above the milky, glistening foam;
515 Whiles all men save the silent helmsman slept,
And once she thought she saw her ancient home.
And every dusk her sisters rose and wept,
And almost to her side the five upclomb.
By signs she told them she was happy still,
520 Beloved of men; and nowise treated ill.

66

The ship reached port; and, in magnificence,
Prince Philo waited for his promised bride.
Days did he wait, in nervous indolence.
At last she came. The Prince's eyes flashed wide
525 With sudden ecstasy; in voice drawn tense
By all the mighty joy of years untried,
And played upon by stroke of present passion,
He chanted (while Philotis' lips grew ashen):

67

"Tis thou! 'Tis thou! Sans whom were I now dead!'
530 And for a while he could nor think nor say,
But even as her little curly head
Was shut between his shoulders quite away,
So in her being, his soul was burièd,
And hidden from the glare of common day.
535 She was indeed the damsel of the sands!
Well, well may poor Philotis wring her hands!

Why should I tell how fine the bridals were,
How many flaming heralds rode the streets,
Or what loud peals went rioting through the air,
540   Or how the towns were choked with wine and meats,
Since Lotis of these things was not aware?
Forlorn Philotis! Scalding chills and heats,
Visions wherein one face did ever melt,
And, with it, worlds, were all she saw and felt.

69

545   'Twas so, though still she danced as she was used,
Danced out and far beyond the reach of Art,
For she forgot her feet were sadly bruised.
Her Prince had said: 'You will rejoice, sweetheart,'
So she forgot her soles were sore contused,
550   Because the sharper pain was at her heart.
Thus the great wedding day came, blazed, and passed,
And fell the night which was to be her last.

70

It found her on his vessel, homeward bound.
Musicians, sailors, revellers, were withdrawn.
555   The sea was tranquil, heaving without sound.
Already, o'er the east, wan chasms yawn.
The passing billows, weltering mound on mound,
Shone ghastly in the doleful light of dawn.
Then saw she how five mermaids rose all pale,
560   To save her, if their plan might aught avail.

71

No more their lovely locks streamed out, wind-fanned.
'We gave them to the witch', they said, 'for this,'
And pressed a dagger in her loathful hand.
'Strike deeply at his heart: it cannot miss.
565   So shalt thou conquer Fate, and Death withstand.
For when his blood shall sprinkle thee, we wis,
Thy feet shall close into a tail once more.
Thus all may be as it hath been before.'

72

So, shrilling, 'Haste!' they sank. And night was spent.
Then she, approaching where the bridegroom slept,
Lifted the scarlet curtain of his tent.
The slumbering pair she saw, and to them crept.
So close they lay, their very curls were blent,
And both her hands beneath his cheek he kept.
Philotis, kneeling, stole her last embrace.
Then turned and watched the sky, a little space.

73

She scanned the coming colour breathlessly,
As 'twere some fateful cauldron, heaving slow.
And now the dull and heavy-clouded sky
Gave forth a steady and increasing glow,
As tarnished lead, that heat doth glorify,
A weird and ruddy brilliancy can throw.
Sudden, like bubble on hot metal seething,
Bulged the great sun. Then ceased Philotis' breathing.

74

Still stood she by the spoiler of her life,
List'ning his dreamy murmurs. What she caught
Was ever one same word: 'Fair wife, sweet wife.'
Ah, She, She only filled his heart and thought!
And Lotis' fingers clutched the raisèd knife.
But ere the fountain of his blood it sought,
It hurtled back, and splashed along the wave,
And she had leapt into the sea: her grave.

75

The sun passed flaming up his azure path,
And warmed the drift of froth that erst was flesh.
She felt the radiance, and as from a bath,
Uprist into the air, ethereal, fresh.
She had not feathers, as an angel hath,
Nor fairy wings of clear and gauzy mesh;
But yet slid upward, like a lifting mist,
And floated, cloudlike, though heaven's amethyst.

76

Around her, floated spirits fair as she.
No fear she felt of their so perfect form,
Nor of their tongues' angelic melody,
Nor of the numbers of that rosy swarm.
605 They told her of their office and degree:
To heal the pestilence; to still the storm;
To fan the atmosphere of fiery regions;
Guide honey-bees, and pilot swallow legions.

77

But what they whispered of her after-fate,
610 The years which this sweet work must see elapse,
Before her final, heavenly estate,
I have not learned. She worketh yet, perhaps;
This evening's sunset may illuminate;
Maybe your garden's tender buds she wraps;
615 Or breathed the scent into the rose you wear,
Or even now, is smiling by your chair.

78

No more than this knows he that told her tale:
That, looking through the vapours under her,
She saw the ocean, and one lonely sail.
620 On board was weeping and unwonted stir.
Both Philo and his bride were very pale.
She heard his hushed, half-sobbing voice aver:
'Woe! Woe! The child hath cast herself away!'
And kissed them, gazing on the pearly spray.

Written at Dunsden after WO had finished his blank-verse retelling of another of Hans Andersen's tales, 'Little Claus and Big Claus' (CP&F, 17) (WO, 78–80). On 17 September 1912, he wrote to SO: 'The other day I started afresh on *The Little Mermaid* and have done 19 stanzas. Would you like to hear one of the best?' He then quoted a version of stanza 9 (CL, 161). Later that month, he told HO: 'I have now written 30 stanzas of "The Little Mermaid" – and not half done yet' (CL, 74; Letter 82 is there misdated). The poem was probably completed that autumn.

29–30   Cp. Keats, *Endymion*, III. 426–7: 'With . . . honey-words she wove / A net.'

  91   Cp. 'The city lights along the waterside' (p. 82).

111   amain: greatly.

114   Cp. Shelley, 'Adonais', l. 462: 'Life, like a dome of many-coloured glass'.

119–20   Cp. Coleridge, *Ancient Mariner*, ll. 53–4: 'And ice, mast-high, came floating by, / As green as emerald.'

153   Cp. Coleridge, *Ancient Mariner*, l. 93: 'For all averred, I had killed the bird.'

164–6   Cp. Coleridge, *Ancient Mariner*, ll. 129–30: 'The water, like a witch's oils, / Burnt green, and blue and white.'

196   Titania: Queen of the fairies. See *A Midsummer Night's Dream*.

226   Cp. Coleridge, *Ancient Mariner*, ll. 97–8: 'Nor dim nor red, like God's own head, / The glorious Sun uprist.'

230   Cp. Keats, 'Isabella', xxxv: 'the forest tomb / Had marred his glossy hair.'

356–9   Cp. Spenser, *Faerie Queene*, I. i. 15: 'Of her there bred / A thousand yong ones, which she dayly fed, / Sucking upon her poisonous dugs.'

395   cist: sepulchral chamber.

397   Cp. Keats, 'To Homer', l. 7: 'And Neptune made for thee a spumy tent.'

415   chyle: digestive juices.

439   amate: daunted.

447   Cp. Coleridge, *Ancient Mariner*, l. 227: 'the ribbed sea-sand'.

493   I had as lieve [lief]: I would as gladly.

566   wis: know.

CP&F, 205

THE TWO REFLECTIONS

I seldom look into thy brown eyes, child,
But I behold in them the deep, cool shade
Of summer woods. Hence always, if dismayed
To think how quickly Time hath us beguiled
5   Of those enchanted days, when forest-wild,
We roamed the copses, and so gaily played;
I feel about me yet the dusky glade,
And June's late light through long lanes, beechen-aisled.
And in the glistening of thy fragrant hair
10 Sparkles the scented rain that glistened then.
But ah! I see, too, thou being otherwhere,
Thy shadowy eyes in every low-lit glen;
Thy locks in every sun-gilt shower, and there
In those sweet glooms, find sorrow unaware.

Written probably in autumn 1912, this poem may be a recollection of the river trip described in WO's letter of 27 June 1912 to MO: 'For tea, we moored up against a beech-wooded escarpment, miles long, on the left bank. I and three élite, adventuresome children climbed to the top; and came down at a breathless rate. . . . We reached Caversham about 7.30; and I of course rode home; but I thought of two little feet that had to walk, even to beyond the Vicarage, and was troubled.' (CL, 145) The 'two little feet' were probably those of 'mine own favourite Milly [Montague]'.

CP&F, 207

[DEEP UNDER TURFY GRASS]

Deep under turfy grass and heavy clay
They laid her bruisèd body, and the child.
Poor victims of a swift mischance were they,
Adown Death's trapdoor suddenly beguiled.
5   I, weeping not, as others, but heart-wild,
Affirmed to Heaven that even Love's fierce flame
Must fail beneath the chill of this cold shame.

So I rebelled, scorning and mocking such
As had the ignorant callousness to wed
10 On altar steps long frozen by the touch
Of stretcher after stretcher of our dead.
Love's blindness is too terrible, I said;
I will go counsel men, and show what bin
The harvest of their homes is gathered in.

15 But as I spoke, came many children nigh,
Hurrying lightly o'er the village green;
Methought too lightly, for they came to spy
Into their playmate's bed terrene.
They clustered round; some wondered what might mean
20 Rich-odoured flowers so whelmed in fetid earth;
While some Death's riddle guessed ere that of Birth.

And there stood one Child with them, whose pale brows
Wore beauty like our mother Eve's; whom seeing,
I could not choose but undo all my vows,
25 And cry that it were well that human Being
And Birth and Death should be, just for the freeing
Of one such face from Chaos' murky womb,
For Hell's reprieve is worth not this one bloom.

Written at Dunsden between late October 1912 and June 1913. On 15 October
1912, WO had assisted at the double funeral of Alice Mary Allen and her
four-year-old daughter, Hilda Agnes (WO, 80–1).

CP&F, 208

[UNTO WHAT PINNACLES]

Unto what pinnacles of desperate heights
Do good men climb to seize their good!
What abnegation to all mortal joys,
What vast abstraction from the world is theirs!
5   O what insane abuses, desperate pangs,
Annihilations of the Self, soul-suicides,
They wreak upon themselves to purchase – GOD!
A God to guide through these poor temporal days
Their comings, goings, workings of the heart,
10 Obsess, indeed, their natures utterly;
Meanwhile preparing, as in recompense,
Mansions celestial for their timeless bliss.
And to what end this Holiness; this God
That arrogates their intellect and soul?
15 To none! Their offered lives are not so grand,
So active, or so sweet as many a one's
That is undedicate, being reason-swayed;
And their sole mission is to drag, entice
And push mankind to those same cloudy crags
20 Where they first breathed the madness-giving air
That made them feel as angels, that are less than men.

Completed at Dunsden on 6 November 1912, according to the dated MS
(WO, 81–2).

CP&F, 209

SONNET

Daily I muse on her; I muse and fret;
And take her little face between each hand;
But spare her – even imagined – kisses yet.
It is because, when first that face I scanned,
5   It wakened doubts I may no more forget,
And curious dreads I cannot understand.
They reach beyond the fears fond lovers pet,
That faith may change ere death; for they demand:

'What of her after Death? Shall we persist?
10 Will Death be merciful and keep her whole?'
In wonderment at this, I have not kissed;
And even now methought a whisper stole:
'Hast thou so learned Love's Law, and yet not wist
Her Beauty lives not? How, then, can her Soul?'

Written at Dunsden on 9 January 1913. One draft is dated 'Jan 9. 1912', but since it is on the same paper and in the same ink as a draft of 'On My Songs' (p. 90), dated 'Jan 4 191³,', it seems reasonable to assume that the other date should have been similarly emended. The subject of the poem is almost certainly a young Dunsden girl.

4 Cp. Shakespeare, Sonnet 104, l. 2: 'when first your eye I ey'd'.
11 Cp. 'The Sleeping Beauty' (p. 81), ll. 11–14:
    So back I drew tiptoe from that Princess,
    Because it was too soon, and not my part,
    To start voluptuous pulses in her heart,
    And kiss her to the world of Consciousness.

CP&F, 210

URICONIUM
An Ode

It lieth low near merry England's heart
Like a long-buried sin; and Englishmen
Forget that in its death their sires had part.
And, like a sin, Time lays it bare again
5   To tell of races wronged,
And ancient glories suddenly overcast,
And treasures flung to fire and rabble wrath.
      If thou hast ever longed
To lift the gloomy curtain of Time Past,
10   And spy the secret things that Hades hath,
Here through this riven ground take such a view.
The dust, that fell unnoted as a dew,
Wrapped the dead city's face like mummy-cloth:
All is as was: except for worm and moth.

Since Jove was worshipped under Wrekin's shade
15   Or Latin phrase was writ in Shropshire stone,
Since Druid chaunts desponded in this glade
Or Tuscan general called that field his own,
      How long ago? How long?
How long since wanderers in the Stretton Hills
20   Met men of shaggy hair and savage jaw,
      With flint and copper prong,
Aiming behind their dikes and thorny grilles?
      Ah! those were days before the axe and saw,
25   Then were the nights when this mid-forest town
      Held breath to hear the wolves come yelping down,
      And ponderous bears 'long Severn lifted paw,
      And nuzzling boars ran grunting through the shaw.

Ah me! full fifteen hundred times the wheat
30   Hath risen, and bowed, and fallen to human hunger
Since those imperial days were made complete.
The weary moon hath waxen old and younger
      These eighteen thousand times
Without a shrine to greet her gentle ray.
35   And other temples rose; to Power and Pelf,

And chimed centurial chimes
Until their very bells are worn away.
While King by King lay cold on vaulted shelf
And wars closed wars, and many a Marmion fell,
40 And dearths and plagues holp sire and son to hell;
And old age stiffened many a lively elf
And many a poet's heart outdrained itself.

I had forgot that so remote an age
Beyond the horizon of our little sight,
45 Is far from us by no more spanless gauge
Than day and night, succeeding day and night,
          Until I looked on Thee,
Thou ghost of a dead city, or its husk!
But even as we could walk by field and hedge
50   Hence to the distant sea
So, by the rote of common dawn and dusk,
We travel back to history's utmost edge.
Yea, when through thy old streets I took my way,
And recked a thousand years as yesterday,
55 Methought sage fancy wrought a sacrilege
To steal for me such godly privilege!

For here lie remnants from a banquet table –
Oysters and marrow-bones, and seeds of grape –
The statement of whose age must sound a fable;
60 And Samian jars, whose sheen and flawless shape
          Look fresh from potter's mould.
Plasters with Roman finger-marks impressed;
Bracelets, that from the warm Italian arm
          Might seem to be scarce cold;
65 And spears – the same that pushed the Cymry west –
Unblunted yet; with tools of forge and farm
Abandoned, as a man in sudden fear
Drops what he holds to help his swift career:
For sudden was Rome's flight, and wild the alarm.
70 The Saxon shock was like Vesuvius' qualm.

O ye who prate of modern art and craft
Mark well that Gaulish brooch, and test that screw!

Art's fairest buds on antique stem are graft.
Under the sun is nothing wholly new!
75   At Viricon today
The village anvil rests on Roman base
And in a garden, may be seen a bower
       With pillars for its stay
That anciently in basilic had place.
80 The church's font is but a pagan dower:
A Temple's column, hollowed into this.
So is the glory of our artifice,
Our pleasure and our worship, but the flower
Of Roman custom and of Roman power.

85 O ye who laugh and, living as if Time
Meant but the twelve hours ticking round your dial,
Find it too short for thee, watch the sublime,
Slow, epochal time-registers awhile,
       Which are Antiquities.
90 O ye who weep and call all your life too long
And moan: Was ever sorrow like to mine?
       Muse on the memories
That sad sepulchral stones and ruins prolong.
Here might men drink of wonder like strong wine
95 And feel ephemeral troubles soothed and curbed.
Yet farmers, wroth to have their laws disturbed,
Are sooner roused for little loss to pine
Than we are moved by mighty woes long syne.

Above this reverend ground, what traveller checks?
100 Yet cities such as these one time would breed
Apocalyptic visions of world-wrecks.
Let Saxon men return to them, and heed!
       They slew and burnt,
But after, prized what Rome had given away
105 Out of her strength and her prosperity.
       Have they yet learnt
The precious truth distilled from Rome's decay?
Ruins! On England's heart press heavily!
For Rome hath left us more than walls and words

110 And better yet shall leave; and more than herds
Or land or gold gave the Celts to us in fee;
E'en Blood, which makes poets sing and prophets see.

Written, probably at Shrewsbury, in July 1913 (WO, 88–90). Since August 1909, and perhaps earlier, WO had been a fascinated explorer of the remains of Uriconium, the Roman city at Wroxeter, on the Severn, east of Shrewsbury. The city and its inhabitants were destroyed by fire and sword c. A.D. 400. The first excavations were carried out in 1859–61, and the more important finds placed in the Shrewsbury Museum. WO and HO themselves collected several boxes full of shards. 'Uriconium / An Ode' owes a good deal to WO's copy of George Fox's *Guide to the Roman City of Uriconium* (1911).

15 Wrekin's shade: The Wrekin is a hill ten miles to the east of Shrewsbury.

28 shaw: thicket or small wood.

39 Marmion: Lord Marmion, the hero of Scott's poem, *Marmion / A Tale of Flodden Field* (1808), was killed at the battle of Flodden in 1513.

63 Cp. Keats, 'The Eve of St. Agnes', l. 228: 'Unclasps her warméd jewels one by one'.

65 the Cymry: the Welsh.

70 Vesuvius' qualm: WO owned a copy of Bulwer-Lytton's *The Last Days of Pompeii* (1834), and in January 1909 wrote a lurid school essay on the subject of earthquakes and volcanic eruptions.

91 Cp. Herbert, 'The Sacrifice', l. 4: 'Was ever grief like mine?'

[WHEN LATE I VIEWED THE GARDENS]

When late I viewed the gardens of rich men,
Where throve my darling blossoms plenteously,
With others whose rare glories dazed my ken,
I was not teased with envious misery.
5 Enough for me to see and recognize;
Then bear away sweet names upon my tongue,
Scents in my breath, and colours in my eyes.
Their owners watch them die: I keep them young.

But when more spacious pleasances I trod,
10 And saw their thousand buds, but might not kiss
Though loving like a lover, sire, and God,
Sad was the yearning of my avarice.
The rich man gives his parting guest one bloom,
But God hath vouchsafed my meek longing – whom?

Written in July–August 1913. Despite the disclaimer in WO's letter of
mid-August 1913 to ELG that his sonnet 'was writ <u>before Meols</u>' (CL, 193), it
clearly owes something to the handsome house and garden of his uncle Edward
Quayle.

    11 Cp. WO to SO, 29 January 1913: 'I can experience the happiness of
       paternity, fraternity, and amativeness all in one, sometimes' (CL, 180).

CP&F, 211

[LONG AGES PAST]

Long ages past in Egypt thou wert worshipped
And thou wert wrought from ivory and beryl.
They brought thee jewels and they brought their slain,
Thy feet were dark with blood of sacrifice.
5 From dawn to midnight, O my painted idol,
Thou satest smiling, and the noise of killing
Was harp and timbrel in thy pale jade ears;
The livid dead were given thee for toys.

Thou wert a mad slave in a Persian palace,
10 And the King loved thee for thy furious beauty,
And all men heard thy ravings with a smile
Because thy face was fairer than a flower.
But with a little knife so wantonly
Thou slewest women and thy pining lovers,
15 And on thy lips the stain of crimson blood,
And on thy brow the pallor of their death.

Thou art the dream beheld by frenzied princes
In smoke of opium. Thou art the last fulfilment
Of all the wicked, and of all the beautiful.
20 We hold thee as a poppy to our mouths,
Finding with thee forgetfulness of God.
Thou art the face reflected in a mirror
Of wild desire, of pain, of bitter pleasure.
The witches shout thy name beneath the moon,
25 The fires of Hell have held thee in their fangs.

Fair-copied, according to the MS, on 31 October 1914 (wo, 111), this poem,
notes Welland (42–3), 'is an invocation to an unspecified deity whose
associations with passion, blood, and violent death prompt in the poet a frenzied
exultation at this fusion of beauty and sin. Such, at least, seems to have been the
intention, but the real motivation behind the poem seems to have been only a
surfeit of Swinburne and Wilde, as is apparent from the heavily-accented
alliteration, the reliance on a naïvely-employed sensuous imagery that recalls
Wilde's "The Sphinx", and such phrases as "furious beauty", "wild desire",
and "bitter pleasure".'

CP&F, 212

[O WORLD OF MANY WORLDS]

O World of many worlds, O life of lives,
    What centre hast thou? Where am I?
O whither is it thy fierce onrush drives?
    Fight I, or drift; or stand; or fly?

5   The loud machinery spins, points work in touch;
    Wheels whirl in systems, zone in zone.
Myself, having sometime moved with such,
    Would strike a centre of mine own.

Lend hand, O Fate, for I am down, am lost!
10   Fainting by violence of the Dance . . .
Ah thanks, I stand – the floor is crossed,
    And I am where but few advance.

I see men far below me where they swarm . . .
    (Haply *above* me – be it so!
15   Does space to compass-points conform,
    And can we say a star stands high or low?)

Not more complex the millions of the stars
    Than are the hearts of mortal brothers;
As far remote as Neptune from small Mars
20   Is one man's nature from another's.

But all hold course unalterably fixed;
    They follow destinies foreplanned:
I envy not these lives their faith unmixed,
    I would not step with such a band.

25   To be a meteor, fast, eccentric, lone,
    Lawless; in passage through all spheres,
Warning the earth of wider ways unknown
    And rousing men with heavenly fears . . .

This is the track reserved for my endeavour;
30   Spanless the erring way I wend.

Blackness of darkness is my meed for ever?
    And barren plunging without end?

O glorious fear! Those other wandering souls
    High burning through that outer bourne
35 Are lights unto themselves. Fair aureoles
    Self-radiated there are worn.

And when in after times those stars return
    And strike once more earth's horizon,
They gather many satellites astern,
40   For they are greater than this system's Sun.

Begun at Dunsden, probably late in 1912, and continued in France between October and December 1914. 'Perhaps the Vicar [of Dunsden] drew Owen's attention to St. Jude's ferocious condemnation of heretical and worldly men within the Church who were "Raging waves of the sea, foaming out their own shame; wandering stars, to whom is reserved the blackness of darkness for ever"' (DH, 31). WO quoted this passage from Jude 13 in his letter of 26 April 1913 to SO: 'the Telescope I luckily gave to Colin acted as a talisman, potent as the Arabian Magician's Ivory Rod. For by feigning to see strange things through it (as indeed I did if mist and the blackness-of-darkness-for-ever are strange) I gathered five gentle children about me. . . .' (CL, 187)

   1 Cp. Shelley, 'O World, O Life, O Time'; and Tagore, *Gitanjali*, poem 12,
      ll. 3–6:
          I came out on the chariot of the first
        gleam of light, and pursued my voyage
        through the wilderness of worlds, leaving
        my track on many a star and planet.
  11 the floor: Cp. Keats, 'The Fall of Hyperion', l. 234: 'the pavèd floor'.
  25 meteor: Cp. WO to SS, 5 November 1917: 'And you have <u>fixed</u> my Life –
      however short. You did not light me: I was always a mad comet; but you
      have fixed me. I spun round you a satellite for a month, but I shall swing
      out soon, a dark star in the orbit where you will blaze. It is some
      consolation to know that Jupiter himself sometimes swims out of Ken!'
      (CL, 505)
33–6 Cp. Shelley, 'Adonais', ll. 492–5:
      I am born darkly, fearfully, afar;
        Whilst burning through the inmost veil of Heaven,
        The soul of Adonais, like a star,
      Beacons from the abode where the Eternal are.

CP&F, 213

[THE TIME WAS AEON]

The time was aeon; and the place all earth.
The spectacle I saw was not a dream,
But true resumption of experienced things.
The scene meseemed one vast deformity,
5   Made lovely by pervasion of a spirit.
For as the morning sunshine sanctifies
Even the ordure of a sordid town,
So all this wreck was glamoured by some charm
A mystery of music. For, a Presence there
10   Created low, rich music, endlessly.
The Place was called the World, and lo! the name
Of him, the unapparent spirit, was
An evil Angel's; and I learnt the name
Of that strange, regnant Presence as the Flesh.
15   It bore the naked likeness of a boy
Flawlessly moulded, fine exceedingly,
Beautiful unsurpassably – so much
More portraiture were fond futility
For even thought is not long possible,
20   Becoming too soon passion: and meseemed
His outline changed, from beauty unto beauty,
As change the contours of slim, sleeping clouds.
His skin, too, glowed, pale scarlet like the clouds
Lit from the eastern underworld; which thing
25   Bewondered me the more. But I remember
The statue of his body standing so
Against the huge disorder of the place
Resembled a strong music; and it triumphed
Even as the trend of one clear perfect air
30   Across confusion of a thousand chords.
Then watched I how there ran towards that way
A multitude of railers, hot with hate,
And maddened by the voice of a small Jew
Who cried with a loud voice, saying 'Away!
35   Away with him!' and 'Crucify him! Him,
With the affections and the lusts thereof.'

Begun, probably at Dunsden, in 1912/13 (WO, 70–1); a heavily corrected fair copy headed 'Final Version' was made at Mérignac in summer 1915. 'The small Jew is St. Paul, urging his followers to "crucify the flesh" (Galatians 5: 24). It is clear from the passionate tone of the description that the poet's sympathies lie entirely with "the Flesh" and not at all with St Paul.' (DH, *Wilfred Owen* [Writers and Their Work, 1975], 10) 'Read out of context, this clumsy and over-written piece might be taken as some kind of homosexual fantasy. It becomes less odd, however, when it is recognized as an imitation of [Harold] Monro's prophetic style and a reworking of the symbolic "Titan of the dawn – Humanity" which is described in the opening poem of *Before Dawn*:

> His visionary eyes looked out afar
>   Beyond the transient semblances of death.
> No sound of supplication came to mar
>
> The rhythm of his calmly-taken breath.
>   No ripple of a thin or faint delight
> Moved round his crimson lips; and underneath
>
> His bright skin aureoled by the rose twilight
>   Rolled the vast torrent of majestic thews.
> Master of his strong passion . . .'

(DH, 'Wilfred Owen and the Georgians', RES, n.s., xxx, no. 117 [1979], 28–40)

21 Cp. Wesley, 'Love Divine, all loves excelling', ll. 21–2: 'changed from glory into glory, / Till in heaven we take our place. . . .'

CP&F, 216

NOCTURNE

Now, as the warm approach of honied slumber blurs my sense,
Before I yield me to th'enchantment of my bed,
God rest all souls in toil and turbulence,
All men a-weary seeking bread;
5   God rest them all tonight!
Let sleep expunge
The day's monotonous vistas from their sight;
And let them plunge
Deep down the dusky firmament of reverie
10 And drowse of dreams with me.

Ah! I should drowse away the night most peacefully
But that there toil too many bodies unreposed
Who fain would fall on lethargy;
Too many leaden eyes unclosed;
15 And aching hands amove
Interminably,
Beneath the light that night will not remove;
Too many brains that rave in dust and steam!
They rave, but cannot dream!

Written at Mérignac between June and August 1915.

CP&F, 217

[52]

IMPROMPTU

Now, let me feel the feeling of thy hand –
For it is softer than the breasts of girls,
And warmer than the pillows of their cheeks,
And richer than the fullness of their eyes,
5   And stronger than the ardour of their hearts.

Its shape is subtler than a dancer's limbs;
Its skin is coloured like the twilight Alp;
And odoured like the pale, night-scented flowers,
And fresh with early love, as earth with dawn.

10   Yield me thy hand a little while, fair love;
That I may feel it; and so feel thy life,
And kiss across it, as the sea the sand,
And love it, with the love of Sun for Earth.

Ah! let me look a long while in thine eyes,
15   For they are deeper than the depths of thought,
And clearer than the ether after rain,
And suaver than the moving of the moon,
And vaster than the void of all desire.

Child, let me fully see and know those eyes!
20   Their fire is like the wrath of shaken rubies;
Their shade is like the peaceful forest-heart.

They hold me as the great star holds the less.
I see them as the lights beyond this life.
They reach me by a sense not found in man,
25   And bless me with a bliss unguessed of God.

Written in Bordeaux between June and August 1915; ll. 1–13 were incorporated
in a letter to ELG (CL, 343–4).

    6–9 Cp. 'From My Diary, July 1914' (p. 97).

CP&F, 218

[53]

A PALINODE

Some little while ago, I had a mood
When what we know as 'Nature' seemed to me
So sympathetic, ample, sweet, and good
That I preferred it to Society.

5   Not for a season, be it understood,
But altogether and perpetually.
As far as feeling went, I thought I could
Be quit of men, live independently.

For men and minds, heart-humours and heart's-tease
10   Disturbed without exciting: whereas woods,
The seasonal changes, and the chanting seas
Were both soul-rousing and sense-lulling. Moods,

Such moods prolonged, became a mania.
I found the stark stretch of a bleak-blown moor
15   Least barren of all places. Mere extranea
Seemed populace and town: things to ignore.

But if the sovereign sun I might behold
With condescension coming down benign,
And blessing all the field and air with gold,
20   Then the contentment of the world was mine.

In secret deserts where the night was nude
And each excited star grew ardent-eyed,
I tasted more than this life's plenitude,
And far as farthest stars perceive, I spied.

25   Once, when the whiteness of the spectral moon
Had terrorized the creatures of the wold,
When that long staring of the glazed-eyed
Had stupefied the land and made it cold,

I fell seduced into a madness; for,
30   Forgetting in that night the life of days,

I said I had no need of fellows more,
I madly hated men and all their ways.

I hated, feeling hated; I supposed
That others did not need me any more.
35 The book of human knowledge I then closed;
Passion, art, science? Trifles to ignore.

But in my error, men ignored not me,
And did not let me in my moonbeams bask.
And I took antidotes; though what they be
40 Unless yourself be poisoned, do not ask.

For I am overdosed. The City now
Holds all my passion; these my soul most feels:
Crowds surging; racket of traffic; market row;
Bridges, sonorous under rapid wheels;

45 Pacific lamentations of a bell;
The smoking of the old men at their doors;
All attitudes of children; the farewell
And casting-off of ships for far-off shores.

Written, or at any rate fair-copied, in London in October 1915. The wording of
ll. 37–40 would appear to indicate a sexual awakening behind the change of
heart that occasions the palinode ('Poem in which author retracts thing said in
former poem, recantation', *SOED*).

11 Cp. John Drinkwater, 'The Fires of God', v, l. 164: 'And the great hills
and solemn chanting seas'.

19 Cp. 'Spring Offensive' (p. 169), l. 15. The evolution of the
phrase 'blessed with gold' is discussed in WO, 44.

25 Cp. Meredith, *Modern Love*, xxxix: 'God, what a dancing spectre seems
the moon.' WO had been given a copy of Meredith's *Poems* (1910) in May
1912 (CL, 136 and 141).

27 Cp. 'Perseus' (CP&F, 464), and 'Supposed Confessions of a Secondrate
Sensitive Mind in Dejection' (p. 11), ll. 20–1.

44–5 These lines were incorporated with only slight changes in 'I know
the music' (p. 178). Cp. Flaubert, *Madame Bovary*, part II, chap. VI:
'et la cloche, sonnant toujours, continuait dans les airs sa
lamentation pacifique'.

[IT WAS A NAVY BOY]

It was a navy boy, so prim, so trim,
That boarded my compartment of the train.
    I shared my cigarettes and books to him.
    He shared his heart to me. (Who knows my gain!)

5   (His head was golden like the oranges
That catch their brightness from Las Palmas sun.)
    'O whence and whither bound, lad?' 'Home,' he says,
    'Home, from Hong Kong, sir, and a ten months' run.'

(His blouse was all as blue as morning sea,
10 His face was fresh like dawn above that blue.)
    'I got one letter, sir, just one,' says he,
    'And no shore-leave out there, sir, for the crew.'

(His look was noble as a good ship's prow
And all of him was clean as pure east wind.)
15   'I am no "sir", I said, 'but tell me now
    What carried you? Not tea, nor tamarind?'

Strong were his silken muscles hiddenly
As under currents where the waters smile.
    'Nitre we carried. By next week maybe
20   That should be winning France another mile.'

His words were shapely, even as his lips,
And courtesy he used like any lord.
    'Was it through books that you first thought of ships?'
    'Reading a book, sir, made me go aboard.

25 'Another hour and I'll be home,' he said.
(His eyes were happy even as his heart.)
    'Twenty-five pounds I'm taking home,' he said,
    'It's five miles there; and I shall run, best part.'

And as we talked, some things he said to me
30 Not knowing, cleansed me of a cowardice,
      As I had braced me in the dangerous sea.
      Yet I should scarce have told it but for this.

'Those pounds,' I said. 'You'll put some twenty by?'
'All for my mother, sir.' And turned his head.
35   'Why all?' I asked, in pain that he should sigh:
      'Because I must. She needs it most,' he said.

Written in London in late October or early November 1915.

   19   nitre: sodium nitrate, a chemical component of certain explosives.

CP&F, 219

[WHEREAS MOST WOMEN LIVE]

Whereas most women live this difficult life
Merely in order not to die the death
And take experience as they take their breath,
Accepting backyards, travail, crusts, all naïf;
5   And nothing greatly love, and nothing loathe –
Others there are who seemingly forget
That men build walls to shelter from the wet,
For sustenance take meals, for comfort clothe.

These must embellish every act with grace;
10 These eat for savours; dress to show their lace;
Suppose the earth for gardens; hands for nard.
Now which you hold as higher than the other
Depends, in fine, on whether you regard
The poetess as nobler than the Mother.

Probably written in 1915, this sonnet exists only in a transcript from a MS since lost.

Transcript, CP&F, 222

A NEW HEAVEN
(To —— on Active Service)

Seeing we never found gay fairyland
   (Though still we crouched by bluebells moon by moon)
And missed the tide of Lethe; yet are soon
   For that new bridge that leaves old Styx half-spanned;
5   Nor ever unto Mecca caravanned;
   Nor bugled Asgard, skilled in magic rune;
Nor yearned for far Nirvana, the sweet swoon,
   And from high Paradise are cursed and banned;

  – Let's die home, ferry across the Channel! Thus
10   Shall we live gods there. Death shall be no sev'rance.
Weary cathedrals light new shrines for us.
   To us, rough knees of boys shall ache with rev'rence.
Are not girls' breasts a clear, strong Acropole?
  – There our own mothers' tears shall heal us whole.

Written probably at Witley and, according to one dated MS, in September 1916.

TITLE Taken from Revelation 31:1, 'And I saw a new heaven and a new earth:
     for the first heaven and the first earth were passed away.'

DEDICATION The unnamed soldier has not been identified.

   3 Lethe: In Greek mythology, a river through Hades the taste of whose
      waters caused forgetfulness of the past.

   4 Styx: In Greek mythology, the boundary river encircling Hades.

   6 Asgard: In Norse mythology, the abode of the gods, accessible only by
      the bridge Bifrost.

   9 The MS reads: ' – Let's die home, ferry home across the Channel!
      Thus'. I have omitted the second 'home' on the grounds that it is both
      tautological and involves an uncharacteristic expansion of the pentameter
      line.

11–14 An anticipation of 'Anthem for Doomed Youth' (p. 76), ll. 9–12:
        What candles may be held to speed them all?
         Not in the hands of boys but in their eyes
        Shall shine the holy glimmers of goodbyes.
         The pallor of girls' brows shall be their pall.

  13 Acropole: WO introduces the French word for 'Acropolis', the highest,
      and usually fortified, part of a Greek city. He was presumably thinking of
      the Acropolis at Athens, which is built of white marble, but not domed as
      his image would seem to suggest.

CP&F, 222

STORM

His face was charged with beauty as a cloud
  With glimmering lightning. When it shadowed me,
   I shook, and was uneasy as a tree
That draws the brilliant danger, tremulous, bowed.

5   So must I tempt that face to loose its lightning.
   Great gods, whose beauty is death, will laugh above,
   Who made his beauty lovelier than love.
I shall be bright with their unearthly brightening.

  And happier were it if my sap consume;
10 Glorious will shine the opening of my heart;
The land shall freshen that was under gloom;
What matter if all men cry out and start,
And women hide their faces in their shawl,
At those hilarious thunders of my fall?

Written, according to the dated MS, in October 1916 (WO, 139).

12 Cp. Shelley, 'Ode to Liberty', ll. 164–5: 'Men started, staggering with a
    glad surprise, / Under the lightnings of thine unfamiliar eyes.'
14 hilarious: 'WO's poems are full of strange references to laughter. Cp. l. 6
    above and "Strange Meeting" (p. 125), l. 22' (DH, 112).

CP&F, 225

TO THE BITTER SWEET-HEART:
A DREAM

One evening Eros took me by the hand,
And having folded feathers round my head,
Or sleep like feathers, towards a far hope sped,
I groping, for he bade me understand
5 He would soon fill with Yours my other hand –
But when I heard his singing wings expand
My face fell deeply in his shoulder.
Sweet moons we flew thus, yet I waned not older
But in his exquisiteness I flagged, unmanned
10 Till, when his wings were drooping to an end
Feeling my empty hand fulfilled with His,
I knew Love gave himself my passion-friend.
So my old quest of you requited is,
Ampler than e'er I asked of your girl's grace.
15 I shall not ask you more, nor see your face.

Written in France early in 1917.

1 Eros: Cp. 'To Eros' (p. 92).

CP&F, 225

ROUNDEL

In Shrewsbury Town e'en Hercules wox tired,
Tired of the streets that end not up nor down;
Tired of the Quarry, though seats may be hired
     Of Shrewsbury Town.

5 Tired of the tongues that knew not his renown;
Tired of the Quarry Bye-Laws, so admired
By the Salopian, the somnambulant clown.

Weak as a babe, and in like wise attired,
He leaned upon his club; frowned a last frown,
10 And of ineffable boredom, so expired
     In Shrewsbury Town.

Written probably at the Casualty Clearing Station in May 1917 (rather than at Bordeaux in May 1914, as the editors of CL suggest), this rondel appears in a letter to ELG where it is prefaced: 'I thought I would try a Roundel. I find it exceedingly easy to write one without having either emotion or ideas. Thus: Roundel on the Statue of Hercules reposing from his Labours in the Quarry, Shrewsbury.' (CL, 250).

  1 Hercules: Cp. WO's treatment of the combat between Hercules and Antaeus, 'The Wrestlers' (p. 184).

CP&F, 225

[62]

HOW DO I LOVE THEE?

I cannot woo thee as the lion his mate,
With proud parade and fierce prestige of presence;
Nor thy fleet fancy may I captivate
With pastoral attitudes in flowery pleasance;
5 Nor will I kneeling court thee with sedate
And comfortable plans of husbandhood;
Nor file before thee as a candidate. . . .
I cannot woo thee as a lover would.

To wrest thy hand from rivals, iron-gloved,
10 Or cheat them by a craft, I am not clever.
But I do love thee even as Shakespeare loved,
Most gently wild, and desperately for ever,
Full-hearted, grave, and manfully in vain,
With thought, high pain, and ever vaster pain.

Written probably at the Casualty Clearing Station in May 1917, this poem is
mentioned in the postscript to WO's letter to ELG tentatively dated '? late May
1914' by the editors of CL (250–1). The opening page/s of this is/are missing
and internal evidence suggests 1917 as a more likely date.

TITLE Cp. Elizabeth Barrett Browning, *Sonnets from the Portuguese*, 43: 'How do
       I love thee? Let me count the ways.'

Transcript, CP&F, 226

THE FATES

They watch me, those informers to the Fates
Called Fortune, Chance, Necessity, and Death;
Time, in disguise as one who serves and waits,
Eternity as girls of fragrant breath.
5 I know them. Men and Boys are in their pay,
And those I hold my trustiest friends may prove
Agents of Theirs to take me if I stray
From fatal ordinance. If I move, they move –

Escape? There is one unwatched way; your eyes,
10 O Beauty! Keep me good that secret gate!
And when the cordon tightens of the spies
Let the close iris of your eyes grow great.
So I'll evade the vice and rack of age
And miss the march of lifetime, stage by stage.

Written at Craiglockhart on 31 June / 1 July 1917. On 1 July WO wrote to
ELG: 'Late last night I very hastily draughted a Fate sonnet. I had an Idea –
which is almost my Gospel. Can you get it from this? If so, how would you
express it in prose?' (CL, 473). A '2nd Draught' of 'The Fates' followed.

3 one who serves and waits: Cp. Milton, 'When I Consider How My Light
  Is Spent', l. 14: 'They also serve who only stand and wait.'
13–14 Cp. 'Strange Meeting' (p. 125), l. 32: 'To miss the march of this
  retreating world'.

CP&F, 226

HAPPINESS

Ever again to breathe pure happiness,
So happy that we gave away our toy?
We smiled at nothings, needing no caress?
Have we not laughed too often since with Joy?
5 Have we not stolen too strange and sorrowful wrongs
For her hands' pardoning? The sun may cleanse,
And time, and starlight. Life will sing great songs,
And gods will show us pleasures more than men's.

Yet heaven looks smaller than the old doll's-home,
10 No nestling place is left in bluebell bloom,
And the wide arms of trees have lost their scope.
The former happiness is unreturning:
Boys' griefs are not so grievous as youth's yearning,
Boys have no sadness sadder than our hope.

Begun at Abbeville in February 1917, this poem was one of several written on a 'subject' agreed by WO, ELG, and their mutual friend Olwen Joergens (WO, 161–3). For a fuller account of these competitive compositions, see DH, ' "Rival Pieces on a Chosen Theme": A Note on Some of Wilfred Owen's Minor Poems', *Four Decades of Poetry 1890–1930* (Merseyside), i, no. 1 (January 1976), 70–5. WO writes of Miss Joergens's poem 'Happiness' in his letter to SO of 12 February 1917 (CL, 434), and on 25 February he tells his mother: 'My "Happiness" is dedicated to you. It contains perhaps two good <u>lines</u>. Between you an' me the sentiment is all bilge. Or nearly all. But I think it makes a creditable Sonnet. You must not conclude I have misbehaved in any way from the tone of the poem (though you might infer it if you knew the tone of this Town.) On the contrary I have been a very good boy. . . .' (CL, 437). Sometime between late June and August he revised the poem at Craiglockhart, writing to SO on 8 August 1917: '(Not before January 1917 did I write the <u>only lines</u> of mine that carry the stamp of maturity: these:

But the old happiness is unreturning.
Boys have no grief so grievous as youth's yearning;
Boys have no sadness sadder than our hope.)'   (CL, 482)

SONG OF SONGS

Sing me at dawn but only with your laugh:
  Like sprightly Spring that laugheth into leaf;
  Like Love, that cannot flute for smiling at Life.

Sing to me only with your speech all day,
5   As voluble leaflets do. Let viols die.
  The least word of your lips is melody.

Sing me at dusk, but only with your sigh;
  Like lifting seas it solaceth: breathe so,
  All voicelessly, the sense that no songs say.

10   Sing me at midnight with your murmurous heart;
  And let its moaning like a chord be heard
  Surging through you and sobbing unsubdued.

Written sometime between late June and mid-August 1917 (WO, 210–11). On 23 August 1917 WO told ELG of his first meeting with SS: 'Some of my old Sonnets didn't please him at all. But the "Antaeus" he applauded fervently; and a short lyric which I don't think you know "Sing me at morn but only with thy Laugh" he pronounced perfect work, absolutely charming, etc. etc. and begged that I would copy it out for him, to show to the powers that be.' (CL, 486) The poem was printed in *The Hydra*, 1 September 1917, and in May 1918 it received a consolation prize in a lyric competition organized by *The Bookman*. By then, however, WO had outgrown it, writing to SO on 29 May 1918: 'The *Bookman* affair about which you are so kindly importunate was a mere idle joke, an old lyric I condescended to send from Scarboro'' (CL, 554). The poem has marked affinities with 'From My Diary, July 1914' (p. 97).

   1 Cp. Jonson, 'Song: To Celia', l. 1: 'Drink to me only with thine eyes'.

CP&F, 230

[HAS YOUR SOUL SIPPED]

Has your soul sipped
      Of the sweetness of all sweets?
Has it well supped
      But yet hungers and sweats?

5 I have been witness
      Of a strange sweetness,
All fancy surpassing
      Past all supposing.

Passing the rays
10   Of the rubies of morning,
Or the soft rise
      Of the moon; or the meaning
Known to the rose
      Of her mystery and mourning.

15 Sweeter than nocturnes
      Of the wild nightingale
Or than love's nectar
      After life's gall.

Sweeter than odours
20   Of living leaves,
Sweeter than ardours
      Of dying loves.

Sweeter than death
      And dreams hereafter
25 To one in dearth
      Of life and its laughter.

Or the proud wound
      The victor wears
Or the last end
30   Of all wars.

Or the sweet murder
      After long guard
Unto the martyr
      Smiling at God;

35 To me was that smile,
      Faint as a wan, worn myth,
Faint and exceeding small,
      On a boy's murdered mouth.

Though from his throat
40   The life-tide leaps
There was no threat
      On his lips.

But with the bitter blood
      And the death-smell
45 All his life's sweetness bled
      Into a smile.

Written at Craiglockhart in July-August 1917, this would seem to be one of
WO's first experiments in sustained pararhyme. Five of the rhyme words and
'nocturnes' (l. 15) appear in a long list of pararhymes pencilled on the back of a
draft of a fragment, 'The Imbecile' (CP&F, 429), written in Bordeaux in 1913.
On the back of the last MS page of 'Has your soul sipped' WO has written:
'Marlboro' & Other Poems / Chas Sorely'. Sorley's book was published in
January 1916.

CP&F, 232

THE SWIFT
An Ode

When the blue has broken
      Through the pearly heat
And the grass is woken
      By our early feet,
5   Oh, then to be the Lark! – With all his fun
To pelt my mate with gayest kisses,
And mount to laugh away those blisses
In shaking merriment unto the sun!

When the dark is listening
10   And the leaves hang still,
While the glow-worms, glistening,
      Make the keen stars thrill,
Would I might mourn to one lorn Nightingale
And be the solace of her solitude,
15 Speaking my doles all clear and unsubdued
And audible to her, the Nightingale.

But when eve shines lowly,
      And the light is thinned,
And the moon slides slowly
20   Down the far-off wind,
Oh, then to be of all the birds the Swift!
To flit through ether, with elves winging,
Drawn up western fires, in frenzy singing,
Along the breeze to lean and poise and drift!

25   Fine thou art and agile,
      O thou perfect bird,
As an arrow fragile
      By an Eros whirred;
And like a cross-bow in a Cupid's grasp
30 Thy wings are ever stretched, for striking ready;
And like young Love thou'rt frantic and unsteady,
And sure as his thine aim, and keen as Love's thy gasp.

Strung in tautest tension
By the lust of speed,
35 And the mad contention
Of insatiate greed,
Thou suck'st away the intoxicating air,
Trailing a wake of song in trilling bubbles,
Till distance drowns thee. Then thy light wing doubles,
40 And thou art back, – nay vanished now, Oh where?

Down in sharp declension,
Grazing the low pool;
Up in steep ascension
Where the clouds blow cool;
45 And there thou sleepest all the luminous night,
Aloft this hurry and this hunger,
Floating with years that knew thee younger,
Without this nest to feed, this death to fight.

Airily sweeping and swinging,
50 Quivering unstable,
Like a dark butterfly clinging
To the roof-gable,
Art thou not tired of this unceasing round?
Long'st not for rest in mead or bower?
55 Must lose, as spirits lose, the power
To soar again if once thou come to ground?

Waywardly sliding and slinging,
Speed never slacking,
Easily, recklessly flinging,
60 Twinkling and tacking;
– Oh, how we envy thee thy lovely swerves!
How covet we thy slim wings' beauty,
Nor guess what stress of need and duty
So bent thy frame to those slim faultless curves.

65 Dazzlingly swooping and plunging
Into the nest to peep,
Dangerously leaping and lunging –
Hark! how the younglings cheep!

O Swift! If thou art master of the air
70   Who taught thee! Not the joy of flying
But of thy brood: their throttles' crying
Stung thee to skill whereof men yet despair!

Desperately driving and dashing,
      Hissing and shrieking,
75   Breathlessly hurtling and lashing,
      Seeking and seeking,
What knowest thou of grace or dance or song?
Thy cry that ringeth like a lyric,
Is it indeed of joy, a panegyric?
80   No ecstasy is this. By love's pain it rings strong.

O that I might make me
      Pinions like to thine,
Feathers that would take me
      Whither I incline!
85   Yet more thy spirit's tirelessness I crave;
Yet more thy joyous fierce endurance.
If my soul flew with thy assurance,
What fields, what skies to scour! What seas to brave!

Drafted at Dunsden in the early summer of 1912, after WO had proposed to
ELG one evening that they should each write a poem on the subject of 'The
Swift' (wo, 73, and DH, '"Rival Pieces on a Chosen Theme": A Note on Some
of Wilfred Owen's Minor Poems', *Four Decades of Poetry 1890–1930*
[Merseyside], i, no. 1 [January 1976], 70). The poem was revised in Bordeaux
between June and August 1915, and further revised at Craiglockhart in August
1917, probably before WO came under the influence of SS.

CP&F, 234

INSPECTION

'You! What d'you mean by this?' I rapped.
'You dare come on parade like this?'
'Please, sir, it's – ' ' 'Old yer mouth,' the sergeant snapped.
'I takes 'is name, sir?' – 'Please, and then dismiss.'

5   Some days 'confined to camp' he got,
For being 'dirty on parade'.
He told me, afterwards, the damnèd spot
Was blood, his own. 'Well, blood is dirt,' I said.

'Blood's dirt,' he laughed, looking away,
10 Far off to where his wound had bled
And almost merged for ever into clay.
'The world is washing out its stains,' he said.
'It doesn't like our cheeks so red:
Young blood's its great objection.
15 But when we're duly white-washed, being dead,
The race will bear Field Marshal God's inspection.'

Drafted at Craiglockhart in August 1917 and completed in September, this
shows the influence of SS (cp. 'They').

    7 damnèd spot: A reference to *Macbeth*, v. i. 35: 'Out, damnèd spot!' This
       'deliberately recalls the occasion of Lady Macbeth's sleepwalking when
       blood was indeed dirt – the irremovable dirt of guilt – and the
       association is sustained a few lines later by the reference to the washing
       out of stains, but the same image also carries a sacrificial overtone ("Are
       you washed in the Blood of the Lamb?") which anticipates the grim
       irony of the final lines' (Welland, 62).
    15 The whitewashing of military installations, kerbstones, etc., was a form
       of superficial cleaning resented by British troops and the target of much
       sarcasm. 'Pipe clay', a form of white clay, is applied with water to whiten
       soldiers' webbing equipment.

CP&F, 240

WITH AN IDENTITY DISC

If ever I had dreamed of my dead name
High in the heart of London, unsurpassed
By Time for ever, and the Fugitive, Fame,
There taking a long sanctuary at last,

5   I better that; and recollect with shame
How once I longed to hide it from life's heats
Under those holy cypresses, the same
That keep in shade the quiet place of Keats.

Now, rather, thank I God there is no risk
10 Of gravers scoring it with florid screed,
But let my death be memoried on this disc.
Wear it, sweet friend. Inscribe no date nor deed.
But let thy heart-beat kiss it night and day,
Until the name grow vague and wear away.

Drafted on 23 March 1917, a preliminary fair copy of this sonnet accompanied
WO's letter to CO the following day (WO, **175**–6). In this he wrote: 'I will send
you my last Sonnet, which I started yesterday. I think I will address it to you.
Adieu, mon petit. Je t'embrasse.' (CL, 446) The poem was revised at Craiglockhart
in August–September 1917. It shows the influence of Shakespeare's Sonnet
104, 'To me, fair friend, you never can be old', that in March 1917 WO had
copied from memory into the notebook in which he drafted his own, and Keats's
sonnet, 'When I have fears that I may cease to be'. Previous editors print
an earlier version of ll. 4–8 and emendations proposed by SS to ll. 11 and 14.

TITLE A British soldier was issued with three identity discs bearing his name
and number. They were worn on a cord round his neck and, if he was
killed, one was sent to his next of kin.

2 References to Westminster in the MSS indicate that WO had in mind a
memorial in Poets' Corner, Westminster Abbey.

7–8 Keats is buried among cypress trees in the Protestant Cemetery at Rome.

CP&F, 241

THE PROMISERS

When I awoke, the glancing day looked gay;
The air said: Fare you fleetly; you will meet him!
And when the prosp'rous sun was well begun,
I heard a bird say: Sweetly you shall greet him!

5   The sun fell strong and bold upon my shoulder;
It hung, it clung as it were my friend's arm.
The birds fifed on before, shrill-piping pipers,
Right down to town; and there they ceased to charm.

And there I wandered till the noon came soon,
10   And chimed: The time is hastening with his face!
Sly twilight said: I bring him; wait till late!
But darkness harked forlorn to my lone pace.

Written at Craiglockhart, probably between August and October 1917.

CP&F, 245

MUSIC

I have been urged by earnest violins
   And drunk their mellow sorrows to the slake
Of all my sorrows and my thirsting sins.
   My heart has beaten for a brave drum's sake.
5 Huge chords have wrought me mighty: I have hurled
   Thuds of gods' thunder. And with old winds pondered
Over the curse of this chaotic world, –
   With low lost winds that maundered as they wandered.

I have been gay with trivial fifes that laugh;
10 And songs more sweet than possible things are sweet;
And gongs, and oboes. Yet I guessed not half
Life's symphony till I had made hearts beat,
And touched Love's body into trembling cries,
And blown my love's lips into laughs and sighs.

Begun in October 1916, according to a dated MS, this poem was one of several written on a 'subject' agreed by WO, ELG, and their mutual friend Olwen Joergens (WO, 161–2). For a fuller account of these competitive compositions, see DH, '"Rival Pieces on a Chosen Theme": A Note on Some of Wilfred Owen's Minor Poems', *Four Decades of Poetry 1890–1930* (Merseyside), i, no. 1 (January 1976), 70–5. The poem was revised at Craiglockhart, and evidently shown to SS, between August and November 1917. For a discussion of 'Music' and its links with the fragment, 'Nights with the Wind. A Rhapsody' (CP&F, 439), see Bäckman, 129–31.

     6 gods': EB and CDL read 'God's', for which there is no MS authority.

CP&F, 246

What passing-bells for these who die as cattle?
  – Only the monstrous anger of the guns.
  Only the stuttering rifles' rapid rattle
Can patter out their hasty orisons.
5 No mockeries now for them; no prayers nor bells;
    Nor any voice of mourning save the choirs, –
The shrill, demented choirs of wailing shells;
    And bugles calling for them from sad shires.

What candles may be held to speed them all?
10   Not in the hands of boys but in their eyes
Shall shine the holy glimmers of goodbyes.
    The pallor of girls' brows shall be their pall;
Their flowers the tenderness of patient minds,
And each slow dusk a drawing-down of blinds.

Written at Craiglockhart in September–October 1917 (WO, **217**–22). SS helped with the revision of the poem and, on 25 September, WO wrote to SO: 'I send you my two best war Poems. Sassoon supplied the title "Anthem": just what I meant it to be.' (CL, 496)

    1 passing-bells: WO was probably responding to the anonymous Prefatory Note to *Poems of Today: an Anthology* (1916), of which he possessed the December 1916 reprint: 'This book has been compiled in order that boys and girls, already perhaps familiar with the great classics of the English speech, may also know something of the newer poetry of their own day. Most of the writers are living, and the rest are still vivid memories among us, while one of the youngest, almost as these words are written, has gone singing to lay down his life for his country's cause. . . . there is no arbitrary isolation of one theme from another; they mingle and interpenetrate throughout, to the music of Pan's flute, and of Love's viol, and the bugle-call of Endeavour, and the passing-bells of Death.'

    2 Cp. the fragment, 'But I was looking at the permanent stars' (p. 179): 'The monstrous anger of our taciturn guns'.

  6–7 Cp. Keats, 'To Autumn', l. 27: 'Then in a wailful choir the small gnats mourn.'

    7 Cp. WO to SO, 2 April 1916: 'The fifers are worthy to rank with the demented violins that make Queen's Hall to spin round as a top, and with the Cathedral Choir that pierces thro' the heights of heaven' (CL, 388).

8 Cp. the fragment, 'I know the music' (p. 178): 'Bugles that sadden all the evening air'; and the fragment, 'But I was looking at the permanent stars' (p. 179): 'Bugles sang, saddening the evening air.'

10–11 Cp. Yeats, *Poems* (1895), 'The Wanderings of Oisin', II. 69: 'A maiden with soft eyes like funeral tapers'.

10–13 Cp. 'A New Heaven' (p. 59), ll. 11–13:
> Weary cathedrals light new shrines for us.
>> To us, rough knees of boys shall ache with rev'rence.
> Are not girls' breasts a clear, strong Acropole?

14 Cp. Laurence Binyon, 'For the Fallen', ll. 15–16: 'At the going down of the sun and in the morning / We will remember them.' DH notes: 'Drawing down the blinds of a house, now an almost forgotten custom, indicated either that a funeral procession was passing or that there had been a death in the house. It was customary to keep the coffin in the house until taking it to church; it would be placed in the darkened parlour, with a pall and flowers on it and lighted candles nearby. Relatives and friends would enter the room to pay their last respects. The sestet of the poem, in fact, refers to a household in mourning.' (DH, 147)

CP&F, 249

WINTER SONG

The browns, the olives, and the yellows died,
And were swept up to heaven; where they glowed
Each dawn and set of sun till Christmastide.
And when the land lay pale for them, pale-snowed,
5 Fell back, and down the snow-drifts flamed and flowed.

From off your face, into the winds of winter,
The sun-brown and the summer-gold are blowing;
But they shall gleam again with spiritual glinter,
When paler beauty on your brows falls snowing,
10 And through those snows my looks shall be soft-going.

Fair-copied according to the MS on 18 October 1917, the poem is addressed to
Arthur Newboult, the seven-year-old son of Edinburgh friends, the subject also
of the sonnet, 'Sweet is your antique body, not yet young' (p. 106) (WO,
229–30).

> 1 Cp. WO to SO, 18 October 1917: 'Yesterday I did go to Newboults – an
> event you will no doubt hear of. Chubby Cubby had grown, and his face
> altered. But the old gold and olive ensheath him as in Summer.' (CL, 501)

CP&F, 254

SIX O'CLOCK IN PRINCES STREET

In twos and threes, they have not far to roam,
  Crowds that thread eastward, gay of eyes;
Those seek no further than their quiet home,
  Wives, walking westward, slow and wise.

5 Neither should I go fooling over clouds,
    Following gleams unsafe, untrue,
And tiring after beauty through star-crowds,
    Dared I go side by side with you;

Or be you in the gutter where you stand,
10 Pale rain-flawed phantom of the place,
With news of all the nations in your hand,
    And all their sorrows in your face.

Written at Craiglockhart sometime between August and October 1917 (WO, 124).
On 8 August 1917, WO told SO: 'At present I am a sick man in hospital, by
night; a poet, for quarter of an hour after breakfast; I am whatever and whoever
I see while going down to Edinburgh on the tram: greengrocer, policeman,
shopping lady, errand boy, paper-boy, blind man, crippled Tommy, bank-clerk,
carter, all of these in half an hour; next a German student in earnest; then I
either peer over bookstalls in back-streets, or do a bit of a dash down Princes
Street, – according as I have taken weak tea or strong coffee for breakfast' (CL,
480–1).

TITLE Princes Street is one of the main streets of Edinburgh.

    4 wives, walking westward: Gillian Nelson calls attention to this and other
      echoes in the poem of Wordsworth, 'Stepping Westward'.

    6 Cp. Tennyson, 'Merlin and the Gleam', ll. 7–10,
        I am Merlin,
        And *I* am dying,
        I am Merlin
        Who follow The Gleam.
      WO parodied these lines in his letter of 27 November 1917 to SS: 'I am
      Owen; and I am dying. / I am Wilfred; and I follow the Gleam' (CL, 512).

    7 Cp. Yeats, 'When you are old', l. 12, 'And hid his face amid a crowd of
      stars.'

  10–12 Graham Holliday has pointed out the similarity between these lines and
      Cowper's description of the postman in *The Task*, IV. 5–7:

THE ONE REMAINS

I sometimes think of those pale, perfect faces
My wonder has not looked upon, as yet;
And of those others never to be met;
And often pore I on the secret traces
5   Left in my heart, of countenances seen,
And lost as soon as seen, – but which mine eye
Remembers as my old home, or the lie
Of landscapes whereupon my windows lean.

And as for those long known and worshipped long,
10 But now, alas! no longer, and the song
Of voices that have said 'Adieu, we part,'
Their reminiscences would cease my heart,
Except I still hoped find, some time, some place,
All beauty, once for ever, in one face.

Revised either at Craiglockhart in October–November 1917, or at Scarborough
between November 1917 and January 1918, having been drafted some time
earlier.

TITLE Taken from Shelley, *Adonais*, l. 459: 'The One remains, the many change
      and pass.'

CP&F, 256

----

          the herald of a noisy world,
        With spatter'd boots, strapp'd waist, and frozen locks,
        News from all nations lumb'ring at his back.
12 Cp. Yeats, 'When you are old', l. 8, 'And loved the sorrows of your
    changing face.'

CP&F, 255

THE SLEEPING BEAUTY

Sojourning through a southern realm in youth,
I came upon a house by happy chance
Where bode a marvellous Beauty. There, romance
Flew faerily until I lit on truth –
5   For lo! the fair Child slumbered. Though, forsooth,
She lay not blanketed in drowsy trance,
But leapt alert of limb and keen of glance,
From sun to shower; from gaiety to ruth;
Yet breathed her loveliness asleep in her:
10   For, when I kissed, her eyelids knew no stir.
So back I drew tiptoe from that Princess,
Because it was too soon, and not my part,
To start voluptuous pulses in her heart,
And kiss her to the world of Consciousness.

Written at Bagnères sometime between August and October 1914 (WO, 106–7),
and revised either at Craiglockhart in October–November 1917, or at
Scarborough between November 1917 and January 1918.

   2 house: The Villa Lorenzo, home of the Léger family.
   3 Beauty: Nénette Léger.

CP&F, 258

[THE CITY LIGHTS]

The city lights along the waterside
Kindled serene as blessèd candleshine.
The fires of western heaven, far and wide,
Rose like the reredos of a mighty shrine.
5 Slow swung the odorous trees from side to side,
Like censers, twining twilight mist for fume;
And on the mountain, that high altar-tomb,
The sun stood full of wine, blood-sanctified.

Soft, soft as angels mounting starry stairs
10 The smoke upclomb to space; the while a wind
Sung like an organ voicing many prayers.
I, sliding beads, mine errors to rescind,
Of slowly slipping tears, heard God, who cares,   )
Ineffable God, give pardon that I sinned.

Revised either at Craiglockhart in October–November 1917, or at Scarborough
between November 1917 and January 1918, having been drafted some time
earlier.

CP&F, 260

AUTUMNAL

If it be very strange and sorrowful
To scent the first night-frost in autumntide;
If on the moaning eve when Summer died
Men shuddered, awed to hear her burial;
5   And if the dissolution of one rose
(Whereof the future holds unnumbered store)
Engender human tears, – ah! how much more
Sorrows and suffers he whose sense foreknows
The weakening and the withering of a love,
10   The dying of a love that had been dear!
Who feels upon a hand, but late love-warm,
A hardness of indifference, like a glove;
And in the dead calm of a voice may hear
The menace of a drear and mighty storm.

Revised either at Craiglockhart in October–November 1917, or at Scarborough between November 1917 and January 1918, having been drafted some time earlier.

CP&F, 261

THE UNRETURNING

Suddenly night crushed out the day and hurled
Her remnants over cloud-peaks, thunder-walled.
Then fell a stillness such as harks appalled
When far-gone dead return upon the world.

5   There watched I for the Dead; but no ghost woke.
Each one whom Life exiled I named and called.
But they were all too far, or dumbed, or thralled,
And never one fared back to me or spoke.

Then peered the indefinite unshapen dawn
10 With vacant gloaming, sad as half-lit minds,
The weak-limned hour when sick men's sighs are drained.
And while I wondered on their being withdrawn,
Gagged by the smothering Wing which none unbinds,
I dreaded even a heaven with doors so chained.

Drafted in late 1912 or early 1913, this sonnet was revised either at
Craiglockhart in October–November 1917, or at Scarborough between
November 1917 and January 1918. On the back of the earliest sheet of rough
working, WO drafted a letter to the vicar of Dunsden setting out his objections
to 'The Christian Life' (wo, 85–6).

TITLE Cp. 'Happiness' (p. 65), l. 12: 'The former happiness is unreturning.'
    5–8 Cp. Harold Munro, 'God', ll. 25–7:
                  for when the daylight broke,
          And rapturously I called upon his name,
          He was not there, He neither heard nor spoke.
      6 Cp. Verlaine, 'Mon Rêve familier', l. 11: 'Comme ceux des aimés que la
        Vie exila'. WO made an autograph copy of this poem.
    11 Cp. Sir Lewis Morris, *The Epic of Hades* (1879), 'Andromeda', ll. 137–8:
        'the dead dark hour before the dawn / When sick men die'. WO quoted
        from these lines in his letter of January 1912 to MO: 'you know that at 3
        a.m. our life ebbs at its lowest; that is "the hour when sick men die" '
        (CL, 106).

CP&F, 262

PERVERSITY

We all love more the Passed and the To Be
Than actual time, and far things more than near.
Perverse we all are somehow; calling dear
Rather the rare than fair. But as for me,
5   How singular and sad that I should see
More loveliness in Grecian marbles clear
Than modern flesh, to beauty insincere;
Less glory in a man than any tree.

I fall in love with children, elfin fair;
10   Portraits; dark ladies in dark tales antique;
Or instantaneous faces passed in streets.
I know the dim old gods that never were,
Better than men. One friend I love unique,
But now, thou canst not dream I love thee, Keats!

Revised either at Craiglockhart in October–November 1917, or at Scarborough
between November 1917 and January 1918, having been drafted some time
earlier.

   3 Cp. Keats, 'Lamia', II. 69–70: 'He thereat was stung, / Perverse'.
   6 Cp. Keats, Fragment of 'The Castle Builder', ll. 59–61:
        That I should rather love a Gothic waste
        Of eyesight on cinque-coloured potter's clay,
        Than on the marble fairness of old Greece.
   9 Cp. Keats, 'La Belle Dame sans Merci', l. 29: 'elfin grot'.

CP&F, 264

MAUNDY THURSDAY

Between the brown hands of a server-lad
The silver cross was offered to be kissed.
The men came up, lugubrious, but not sad,
And knelt reluctantly, half-prejudiced.
5 (And kissing, kissed the emblem of a creed.)
Then mourning women knelt; meek mouths they had,
(And kissed the Body of the Christ indeed.)
Young children came, with eager lips and glad.
(These kissed a silver doll, immensely bright.)
10 Then I, too, knelt before that acolyte.
Above the crucifix I bent my head:
The Christ was thin, and cold, and very dead:
And yet I bowed, yea, kissed – my lips did cling.
(I kissed the warm live hand that held the thing.)

Probably drafted at Shrewsbury in May/June 1915 (WO, 119–20), a recollection
of 'the Veneration of the Cross', a Roman Catholic rite in which WO may have
participated at Mérignac on Good Friday (not Maundy Thursday) 1914 with the
de la Touche family. This dating is supported by a passage in his letter of 27
December 1914 to SO: 'We made two journeys to church with the bath chair,
and installed both the boys and ourselves in the very sanctuary. An interesting
position for me, all mixed up with the candles, incense, acolytes, chasuble and
such like. . . . I think the efforts of the dear, darling little acolytes to keep awake
was what took most of my attention there'. (CL, 311) The poem was revised
either at Craiglockhart in October–November 1917, or at Scarborough between
November 1917 and January 1918.

CP&F, 265

THE PERIL OF LOVE

As men who call on spirits get response
And woo successfully the coy Unseen,
Deeming the thing amusement for the nonce,
But later, when dark spirits intervene
5   Uncalled, perceive how an invading mind,
Not to be shaken off, compels them serve
Mad promptings; poisons love of life and kind;
Drains force; clogs brain; and flusters nerve:

So I, lightly addressing me to love,
10 Have found too late love's grave significance.
A fierce infatuation, far above
The zeal for fame or fortune, like a trance,
Exhausts my faculties. I am a prey
Of impulse, the marasmus of decay.

Revised either at Craiglockhart in October–November 1917, or at Scarborough
between November 1917 and January 1918, having been drafted some time
earlier.

    14 marasmus: progressive emaciation.

CP&F, 265

THE POET IN PAIN

Some men sing songs of Pain and scarcely guess
Their import, for they never knew her stress.
And there be other souls that ever lie
Begnawed by seven devils, silent. Aye,
5   Whose hearts have wept out blood, who not once spake
Of tears. If therefore my remorseless ache
Be needful to proof-test upon my flesh
The thoughts I think, and in words bleeding-fresh
Teach me for speechless sufferers to plain,
10 I would not quench it. Rather be my part
To write of health with shaking hands, bone-pale,
Of pleasure, having hell in every vein,
Than chant of care from out a careless heart,
To music of the world's eternal wail.

Revised either at Craiglockhart in October–November 1917, or at Scarborough
between November 1917 and January 1918, having been drafted some time
earlier.

9 plain: mourn, complain.

CP&F, 265

[WHITHER IS PASSED]

Whither is passed the softly-vanished day?
It is not lost by seeming spent for aye.
For as no bar of incense fumeth out
But leaveth finer perfume all about,
5   So the sweet hours, though fast they waste away,
In mild Moneta's shrine like odours stray,
And steal on us as, entering there, devout,
We shut the door upon the world without.

And likewise, too, the souls of men are freed.
10 Sweet lives in their consuming sweeter grow,
And larger, and more wholly earth-released.
Not prayer, unfired and faint, the high gods heed,
But the spent essence of a life aglow
Perfumeth heaven with fragrance unsurceased.

Drafted at Shrewsbury, probably in 1911–12, and revised either at Craiglockhart in October–November 1917, or at Scarborough between November 1917 and January 1918.

   1 Cp. Keats, 'To Autumn', l. 25: 'the soft-dying day'.
   6 Moneta: The 'majestic shadow' (her Latin name suggests 'the Admonisher') who, in Keats's 'The Fall of Hyperion', replaces the figure of Mnemosyne – goddess of Memory – who appears to him in the earlier 'Hyperion'.

CP&F, 266

ON MY SONGS

Though unseen Poets, many and many a time,
Have answered me as if they knew my woe,
And it might seem have fashioned so their rime
To be my own soul's cry; easing the flow
5   Of my dumb tears with language sweet as sobs,
Yet are there days when all these hoards of thought
Hold nothing for me. Not one verse that throbs
Throbs with my heart, or as my brain is fraught.

'Tis then I voice mine own weird reveries:
10 Low croonings of a motherless child, in gloom
Singing his frightened self to sleep, are these.
One night, if thou shouldst lie in this Sick Room,
Dreading the Dark thou darest not illume,
Listen; my voice may haply lend thee ease.

Drafted at Dunsden on 4 January 1913 (CL, 175), under the influence of James
Russell Lowell's sonnet, 'To the Spirit of Keats', quoted in WO's letter to SO
of 17 September 1912:
   'Great soul, thou sittest with me in my room,
   Uplifting me with thy vast quiet eyes,
   On whose full orbs with kindly lustre, lies
   The twilight warmth of ruddy ember-gloom.
   Thy clear strong tones will oft bring sudden bloom
   Of hope secure to him who lonely cries,
   Wrestling with the young poet's agonies,
   Neglect and scorn, which seem a certain doom.'   (CL, 160)
WO revised his sonnet either at Craiglockhart in October–November 1917, or at
Scarborough between November 1917 and January 1918.

CP&F, 266

TO ——

Three rompers run together, hand in hand.
The middle boy stops short, the others hurtle:
What bumps, what shrieks, what laughter turning turtle.
Love, racing between us two, has planned
5 A sudden mischief: shortly he will stand
And we shall shock. We cannot help but fall;
What matter? Why, it will not hurt at all,
Our youth is supple, and the world is sand.

Better our lips should bruise our eyes, than He,
10 Rude Love, out-run our breath; you pant, and I,
I cannot run much farther, mind that we
Both laugh with Love; and having tumbled, try
To go forever children, hand in hand.
The sea is rising . . . and the world is sand.

Drafted in London on 10 May 1916 (WO, **138**), this sonnet is almost certainly a
recollection of a day with the de la Touche boys. WO to SO, 23 July 1915: 'I
shall part with the four boys with regret, – with three of them regretfully, with
two of them sorrowfully, and with one of them very sorrowfully indeed' (CL,
348). The dedicatory title was written in pencil on the one MS, probably later
than the poem and with Johnny de la Touche in mind. The sonnet was revised
either at Craiglockhart in October–November 1917, or at Scarborough between
November 1917 and January 1918.

CP&F, 268

TO EROS

In that I loved you, Love, I worshipped you;
In that I worshipped well, I sacrificed.
All of most worth I bound and burnt and slew:
The innocent small things, fair friends and Christ.

5   I slew all falser loves, I slew all true,
For truth is the prime lie men tell a boy.
Glory I cast away, as bridegrooms do
Their splendid garments in their haste of joy.

But when I fell and held your sandalled feet,
10 You laughed; you loosed away my lips; you rose.
I heard the singing of your wings' retreat;
And watched you, far-flown, flush the Olympian snows,
Beyond my hoping. Starkly I returned
To stare upon the ash of all I burned.

Revised either at Craiglockhart in October–November 1917, or at Scarborough
between November 1917 and January 1918, this sonnet was probably drafted
some time earlier. It appears to relate to the crisis of WO's last days at Dunsden
(WO, 84–5).

TITLE   Eros, the Greek god of Love.
       5   Cp. WO to SO, 4 January 1913: 'Murder will out, and I have murdered
           my false creed. If a true one exists, I shall find it. If not, adieu to the still
           falser creeds that hold the hearts of nearly all my fellow men.' (CL, 175)
      12   The ancient Greeks believed the summit of Mount Olympus to be the
           home of the gods.
      14   Cp. WO to SO, 30 July 1917: 'I saw better the supremer beauty of the
           ashes of all your Sacrifices' (CL, 479).

CP&F, 269

1914

War broke: and now the Winter of the world
With perishing great darkness closes in.
The foul tornado, centred at Berlin,
Is over all the width of Europe whirled,
5 Rending the sails of progress. Rent or furled
Are all Art's ensigns. Verse wails. Now begin
Famines of thought and feeling. Love's wine's thin.
The grain of human Autumn rots, down-hurled.

For after Spring had bloomed in early Greece,
10 And Summer blazed her glory out with Rome,
An Autumn softly fell, a harvest home,
A slow grand age, and rich with all increase.
But now, for us, wild Winter, and the need
Of sowings for new Spring, and blood for seed.

Drafted in France in late 1914 (WO, 105), and revised either at Craiglockhart in October–November 1917, or at Scarborough between November 1917 and January 1918.

1 Cp. Shelley, *The Revolt of Islam*, IX. 25: 'This is the winter of the world; – and here / We die.' WO wrote to SO, 18 March 1916: 'Now is the winter of the world. But my life has come already to its month of March.' (CL, 386)

7 The apparent echo of Rupert Brooke's 'red / Sweet wine of youth' is probably fortuitous. His sonnet 'The Dead' was not published until December 1914, and one draft of '1914' is dated 1914.

8 Cp. the later MS draft of 'Asleep' (p. 129), l. 18: 'And finished fields of autumns that are old' (MSS, CP&F, 314).

9 Cp. Keats, 'To Autumn', ll. 23–5:
    Where are the songs of Spring? Aye, where are they?
      Think not of them, thou hast thy music too –
    While barred clouds bloom the soft-dying day.

12 Cp. Shakespeare, Sonnet 97, l. 6: 'The teeming autumn big with rich increase'.

CP&F, 270

PURPLE

Vividly gloomy, with bright darkling glows
Of nebulae and warm, night-shimmering shores!
Stain of full fruits, wines, passions, and the cores
Of all quick hearts! Yet from its deeps there blows
5   Aroma and romance of violets;
Softness of far land, hazed; pacific lift
Of smoke through quiet trees; and that wild drift
Of smoulder when the flare of evening sets.

Solemn, columnar, thunder-throning cloud
10   Wears it so stately that therein the King
Stands before men, and lies in death's hand, proud.
Purest, it is the diamond dawn of spring;
And yet the veil of Venus, whose rose skin,
Mauve-marbled, purples Eros' mouth for sacred sin.

Drafted, according to a dated MS, in September 1916, this poem may have
been the first to be prepared on a 'subject' agreed by WO, ELG, and their
mutual friend Olwen Joergens (wo, 161–3). For a fuller account of these
competitive compositions, see DH, '"Rival Pieces on a Chosen Theme":
'A Note on Some of Wilfred Owen's Minor Poems', *Four Decades of Poetry
1890–1930* (Merseyside), i, no. 1 (January 1976), 70–5. Since purple was WO's
favourite colour, he may have chosen this subject. ELG's poem 'Purple'
appeared in *The Nymph and Other Poems* (1917). WO's sonnet was revised either
at Craiglockhart in October–November 1917, or at Scarborough between
November 1917 and January 1918.

    6 pacific: Cp. 'A Palinode' (p. 54), l. 45, and the fragment, 'I know the
    music' (p. 178): 'pacific lamentations'.

CP&F, 271

ON A DREAM

I leaned, blank-eyed, in lonely thoughtless thought,
Upon the night, athwart my threshold stone;
When there came One with hurried, frightened moan,
With tear-drained eyes, wild hair, and hands distraught,
5   Who fell about my knees, and swift besought
Help and my love, for she was all alone
For love of me; and from her world out-thrown.
I knew that lovely head; her hands I caught;

For hours I felt her lips warm on my cheek,
10 As through the vast void of the dark we fled.
For precious hours her limbs in mine were curled,
Until with utter joy I tried to speak:
And lo! I raved with fever on my bed,
And melancholy dawn bestirred the world.

Revised either at Craiglockhart in October–November 1917, or at Scarborough
between November 1917 and January 1918, this sonnet was probably drafted
some time earlier. Dream and poem clearly owe something to Keats, 'La Belle
Dame sans Merci', and Verlaine, 'Mon Rêve familier'.

CP&F, 273

[STUNNED BY THEIR LIFE'S EXPLOSION]

Stunned by their life's explosion into love
Some men stay deaf and dizzy ever after,
And blindly through the press they grope or shove,
Nor heed they more of sorrowing or laughter.

5   And others, having fixed their hope above,
Chastened and maimed by bitter chastity,
Grow to forget spring flowers, and why the dove
Makes music with her fellow, endlessly.

Ah! pity these were told not that their thirsts
10   Are slaked nor by priest's wine nor lust's outbursts,
But Poesy. They, knowing Verse to be
God's soothest answer to all passion's plea,
And loving beauties writ and wrought of art,
Might yet have kept a whole and splendid heart.

Revised either at Craiglockhart in October–November 1917, or at Scarborough
between November 1917 and January 1918, having been drafted some time
earlier.

    12 soothest: truest.

CP&F, 274

[96]

FROM MY DIARY, JULY 1914

Leaves
  Murmuring by myriads in the shimmering trees.
Lives
  Wakening with wonder in the Pyrenees.
5 Birds
  Cheerily chirping in the early day.
Bards
  Singing of summer, scything through the hay.
Bees
10 Shaking the heavy dews from bloom and frond.
Boys
  Bursting the surface of the ebony pond.
Flashes
  Of swimmers carving through the sparkling cold.
15 Fleshes
  Gleaming with wetness to the morning gold.
A mead
  Bordered about with warbling waterbrooks.
A maid
20 Laughing the love-laugh with me; proud of looks.
The heat
  Throbbing between the upland and the peak.
Her heart
  Quivering with passion to my pressèd cheek.
25 Braiding
  Of floating flames across the mountain brow.
Brooding
  Of stillness; and a sighing of the bough.
Stirs
30 Of leaflets in the gloom; soft petal-showers;
Stars
  Expanding with the starr'd nocturnal flowers.

Drafted either at Craiglockhart in October–November 1917, or at Scarborough
between November 1917 and January 1918, this early exercise in pararhyme is a
recollection of days at the Villa Lorenzo, outside Bagnères-de-Bigorre in the
French Pyrenees (WO, 106, 211). In fact, WO did not reach
Bagnères-de-Bigorre until 31 July 1914, but presumably he dates his 'diary'

THE BALLAD OF MANY THORNS

A Poet stood in parley
  With Carls a-reaping corn.
Quoth one: 'I curse the Barley,
  More sharp than any thorn.'

5 'Although thy hand be torn,
    Ill-spoken was thy curse:
  I swear thou art forsworn,
    If Thistle wound not worse.'

So groaned a footsore Climber,
10   Had scaled the bristly path:
  'What thorns, Sir Carl, Sir Rimer,
    Like these the Thistle hath?'

Behold a wan youth ramble
  With bleeding cheeks forlorn,
15 And moans: 'The wanton bramble,
    It is the keenest thorn.'

Rode by a wounded Warrior
  Deep muttering like a lion:
  'Show me the flesh wound sorrier
20   Than by the barb of Iron!'

Out laughed a man of folly,
  Much wine had made him thick:
  'The jolly, festive Holly
    Deals oft a nasty prick.'

----

entry July, rather than August, to suggest the last days of peace. The poem has
elements in common with 'Song of Songs' (p. 66), and 'Impromptu / Now, let
me feel' (p. 53).

  3–4 These lines have been cancelled in the MS.
    19 A maid: Probably Nénette Léger.

CP&F, 275

25 There hung near by a Jesus
       With crownèd head for scorn.
   'Ah by His brow, who sees us,
       Was any like His thorn?'

   So sighed a leprous Palmer.
30   But when he thought afresh:
   'Perchance His pain was calmer,
       Than this thorn in my flesh.'

   Then cried the gentle Poet:
       'Not one among ye knows:
35 The cruelest thorn, I know it,
       For having kissed the Rose.'

Written or revised at Craiglockhart in October–November 1917, or at
Scarborough between November 1917 and January 1918.

   4 Cp. Anon., 'The Holly and the Ivy': 'The holly bears a prickle / As sharp
     as any thorn.'
35–6 Probably an allusion to Albertina Marie Dauthieu, the nineteen-year-old
     daughter of the publican of The Thistle public house in Milnathort, a
     village near Edinburgh. WO wrote in her autograph book a gallant
     adaptation of a song from the opera *Merrie England*, ending:
         And so I'll have my posy
         Of the fairest flower that blows
         Embower'd by the Thistle
         And accompanied by a Rose.
                     (WO, 231)

CP&F, 277

[I SAW HIS ROUND MOUTH'S CRIMSON]

I saw his round mouth's crimson deepen as it fell,
 Like a sun, in his last deep hour;
Watched the magnificent recession of farewell,
 Clouding, half gleam, half glower,
5 And a last splendour burn the heavens of his cheek.
  And in his eyes
The cold stars lighting, very old and bleak,
 In different skies.

Drafted, probably at Scarborough, in November–December 1917, this poem, or
fragmentary poem, may be a development of the fragment, 'Spells and
Incantation' (p. 181).

 7–8 Cp. Yeats, 'A Dream of Death', l. 9: 'And left her to the indifferent stars
  above.'

CP&F, 277

APOLOGIA PRO POEMATE MEO

I, too, saw God through mud, –
    The mud that cracked on cheeks when wretches smiled.
    War brought more glory to their eyes than blood,
    And gave their laughs more glee than shakes a child.

5 Merry it was to laugh there –
    Where death becomes absurd and life absurder.
    For power was on us as we slashed bones bare
    Not to feel sickness or remorse of murder.

I, too, have dropped off Fear –
10 Behind the barrage, dead as my platoon,
    And sailed my spirit surging light and clear
    Past the entanglement where hopes lay strewn;

And witnessed exultation –
    Faces that used to curse me, scowl for scowl,
15 Shine and lift up with passion of oblation,
    Seraphic for an hour; though they were foul.

I have made fellowships –
    Untold of happy lovers in old song.
    For love is not the binding of fair lips
20 With the soft silk of eyes that look and long,

By Joy, whose ribbon slips, –
    But wound with war's hard wire whose stakes are strong;
    Bound with the bandage of the arm that drips;
    Knit in the webbing of the rifle-thong.

25 I have perceived much beauty
    In the hoarse oaths that kept our courage straight;
    Heard music in the silentness of duty;
    Found peace where shell-storms spouted reddest spate.

Nevertheless, except you share
30 With them in hell the sorrowful dark of hell,
    Whose world is but the trembling of a flare
    And heaven but as the highway for a shell,

You shall not hear their mirth:
    You shall not come to think them well content
35 By any jest of mine. These men are worth
    Your tears. You are not worth their merriment.

Written at Scarborough in November–December 1917 (WO, **250**–2). The final
fair copy is dated 'Nov. 1917', but it is tempting to see the poem as a response to
a remark in Robert Graves's letter *circa* 22 December 1917: 'For God's sake
cheer up and write more optimistically – The war's not ended yet but a poet
should have a spirit above wars' (CL, 596). Graves may have said much the same
to WO earlier.

TITLE SS corrected the faulty Latin grammar of WO's own title, 'Apologia pro
       Poema Mea', which may have been influenced by that of Cardinal
       Newman's *Apologia Pro Vita Sua*.

   1 too: Welland, 67–8, argues convincingly that this is an allusion to
      Graves's poem 'Two Fusiliers':

And have we done with War at last?   By all the misery and loud sound,
Well, we've been lucky devils both,   By a Spring day,
And there's no need of pledge or oath   By Picard clay.
To bind our lovely friendship fast,
By firmer stuff   Show me the two so closely bound
Close bound enough.   As we, by the wet bond of blood,
                                          By friendship, blossoming from mud,
By wire and wood and stake we're bound,   By Death: we faced him, and we found
By Fricourt and by Festubert,   Beauty in Death,
By whipping rain, by the sun's glare,   In dead men breath.

  13 exultation: Cp. Shelley, 'A Defence of Poetry': 'Poetry is a mirror which
      makes beautiful that which is distorted. . . . it exalts the beauty of that
      which is most beautiful, and it adds beauty to that which is most
      deformed; it marries exultation and horror.'
18–20 Cp. ELG, 'L'Amour', published in *The Nymph and Other Poems*
      (November 1917), ll. 1–2: 'Love is the binding of souls together, / The
      binding of lips, the binding of eyes.'
  21 Cp. Keats, 'Ode on Melancholy', l. 22: 'And Joy, whose hand is ever at
      his lips'.

CP&F, 278

LE CHRISTIANISME

So the church Christ was hit and buried
    Under its rubbish and its rubble.
In cellars, packed-up saints lie serried,
    Well out of hearing of our trouble.

5   One Virgin still immaculate
    Smiles on for war to flatter her.
She's halo'd with an old tin hat,
    But a piece of hell will batter her.

Written, probably at Scarborough, in late November or early December 1917.
At the foot of the corrected fair copy WO has written 'Quivières', a village
where he was quartered in April 1917 (wo, **183**), but as Quivières has no
church, his memory may have been at fault.

    1 Cp. 'At a Calvary near the Ancre' (p. 111), ll. 1–2.
    4 Cp. A. E. Housman, 'On Wenlock edge the wood's in trouble', ll. 19–20:
      'Today the Roman and his trouble / Are ashes under Uricon.'
    8 A pun may be intended, 'piece' meaning both fragment and field-gun,
      as opposed to 'the peace of God'.

CP&F, 281

HOSPITAL BARGE

Budging the sluggard ripples of the Somme,
A barge round old Cérisy slowly slewed.
Softly her engines down the current screwed,
And chuckled softly with contented hum,
5   Till fairy tinklings struck their croonings dumb.
The waters rumpling at the stern subdued;
The lock-gate took her bulging amplitude;
Gently from out the gurgling lock she swum.

One reading by that calm bank shaded eyes
10   To watch her lessening westward quietly.
Then, as she neared the bend, her funnel screamed.
And that long lamentation made him wise
How unto Avalon, in agony,
Kings passed in the dark barge which Merlin dreamed.

Written at Scarborough in December 1917, following 'a Saturday night revel in
"The Passing of Arthur"' (EB, 124; see also WO, 248–9). On 10 May 1917, WO
had written to SO: 'I sailed in a steam-tug about 6 miles down the Canal with
another "inmate". The heat of the afternoon was Augustan; and it has probably
added another year to my old age to have been able to escape marching in
equipment under such a sun. The scenery was such as I never saw or dreamed
of since I read the *Fairie Queene.* Just as in the Winter when I woke up lying on
the burning cold snow I fancied I must have died & been pitch-forked into the
Wrong Place, so, yesterday, it was not more difficult to imagine that my dusky
barge was wending up to Avalon, and the peace of Arthur, and where Lancelot
heals him of his grievous wound. But the Saxon is not broken, as we could very
well hear last night. Later, a real thunderstorm did its best to seem terrible, and
quite failed.' (CL, 457)

     2 Cérisy is one and a half miles down the Somme Canal from Gailly where
       WO was a patient in the 13th Casualty Clearing Station.
     9 reading: The poem implies that the speaker was reading Malory, *Morte*
       Darthur, or a later retelling such as Tennyson, 'The Passing of Arthur',
       from *The Holy Grail and Other Poems* (1870). WO bought a copy of the
       latter book in Edinburgh in July 1917.
    12 lamentation: Cp. Tennyson, 'The Passing of Arthur', ll. 361–71:
         Then saw they how there hove a dusky barge,
       Dark as a funeral scarf from stem to stern,

Beneath them; and descending they were ware
That all the decks were dense with stately forms,
Black-stoled, black-hooded, like a dream – by these
Three Queens with crowns of gold: and from them rose
A cry that shivered to the tingling stars,
And, as it were one voice, an agony
Of lamentation, like a wind that shrills
All night in a waste land, where no one comes,
Or hath come, since the making of the world.

14 In November 1917 WO had marked in his copy of Alfred Austin, *Songs of England* (1898), 'The Passing of Merlin', v:
A wailing cometh from the shores that veil
Avilion's island valley; on the mere,
Looms through the mist and wet winds weeping blear
A dusky barge, which, without oar or sail,
Fades to the far-off fields where falls nor snow nor hail.

CP&F, 281

[SWEET IS YOUR ANTIQUE BODY]

Sweet is your antique body, not yet young.
Beauty withheld from youth that looks for youth.
Fair only for your father. Dear among
Masters in art. To all men else uncouth
5   Save me; who know your smile comes very old,
Learnt of the happy dead that laughed with gods;
For earlier suns than ours have lent you gold,
Sly fauns and trees have given you jigs and nods.

But soon your heart, hot-beating like a bird's,
10   Shall slow down. Youth shall lop your hair,
And you must learn wry meanings in our words.
Your smile shall dull, because too keen aware;
And when for hopes your hand shall be uncurled,
Your eyes shall close, being opened to the world.

Written at Craiglockhart, probably (given the diction shared with
'Miners') in December 1917. The child addressed in this sonnet is Arthur
Newboult, the seven-year-old son of Edinburgh friends (WO, 230). In its theme
and phrasing, the poem shows the influence of Wordsworth's ode, 'Intimations
of Immortality from Recollections of Early Childhood'.

   8 fauns (WO wrote 'fawns'): Cp. 'Miners' (p. 112), l. 8.
  11 wry: Cp. 'Miners', l. 15.

CP&F, 284

PAGE EGLANTINE

Nay, light me no fire tonight,
    Page Eglantine;
I have no desire tonight
    To drink or dine;
5   I will suck no briar tonight,
    Nor read no line;
An you be my quire tonight,
    And you my wine.

Written at Scarborough between November 1917 and February 1918, 'Page Eglantine' may be related to the 'privie page' of the fragment, 'Ballad of Lady Yolande' (CP&F, 472).

5 briar: briar pipe.
7 quire: archaic variant of 'choir'.

CP&F, 284

THE RIME OF THE YOUTHFUL MARINER

One knotted a rope with an evil knout,
    And flogged me till I fell;
And he is picking the rope end out
    In a land-locked prison-cell.

5 One tied my wrist with a twisted cord
    While I lay asleep on deck.
But his reward was overboard,
    With the string around his neck.

One bound my mouth with her hands of silk,
10   And drew me backward so.
Her skin that was foul as curdled milk
    Is fouler today, I trow.

One clogged my feet with a heavy wine,
    And my tongue with a tangling drug.
15 But now his tongue is thicker than mine
    And black as any slug.

One bound my thighs with his muscled arm,
    Whose weight was good to bear.
O may he come to no worse harm
20   Than what he wrought me there.

Written at Scarborough between November 1917 and January 1918.

TITLE Cp. Coleridge, *The Rime of the Ancient Mariner.*
    1 knout: A whip for flogging criminals, but incorrectly used by WO as a
       variant form of 'knot'. Cp. 'Mental Cases' (p. 146), l. 26:
       'Picking at the rope-knouts of their scourging'.
    3 picking the rope end out: The picking of oakum (loose fibres from old
       hemp ropes, subsequently used for caulking the seams of ships) was once
       a common form of employment for prisoners.

CP&F, 285

[WHO IS THE GOD OF CANONGATE?]

Who is the god of Canongate?
    I, for I trifle with men and fate.

Art thou high in the heart of London?
    Yea, for I do what is done and undone.

5 *What is thy throne, thou barefoot god?*
    All pavements where my feet have trod.

Where is thy shrine, then, little god?
    Up secret stairs men mount unshod.

Say what libation such men fill?
10   There lift their lusts and let them spill.

Why do you smell of the moss in Arden?
    If I told you, Sir, your look would harden.

What are you called, I ask your pardon?
    I am called the Flower of Covent Garden.

15 *What shall I pay for you, lily-lad?*
    Not all the gold King Solomon had.

How can I buy you, London Flower?
    Buy me for ever, but not for an hour.

When shall I pay you, Violet Eyes?
20   With laughter first, and after with sighs.

But you will fade, my delicate bud?
    No, there is too much sap in my blood.

Will you not shrink in my shut room?
    No, there I'll break into fullest bloom.

Written, probably at Scarborough, between November 1917
and February 1918 (WO, **240–1**).

MY SHY HAND

My shy hand shades a hermitage apart, –
   O large enough for thee, and thy brief hours.
Life there is sweeter held than in God's heart,
   Stiller than in the heavens of hollow flowers.

5   The wine is gladder there than in gold bowls.
   And Time shall not drain thence, nor trouble spill.
Sources between my fingers feed all souls,
   Where thou mayest cool thy lips, and draw thy fill.

Five cushions hath my hand, for reveries;
10   And one deep pillow for thy brow's fatigues;
Languor of June all winterlong, and ease
   For ever from the vain untravelled leagues.

Thither your years may gather in from storm,
And Love, that sleepeth there, will keep thee warm.

Drafted at Craiglockhart in August 1917 and revised at Scarborough in January–February 1918, this sonnet shows the influence of Yeats's 'To an Isle in the Water' (WO, 212–13).

CP&F, 286

1 and 14 Canongate and Covent Garden are districts of Edinburgh and London, respectively.

CP&F, 285

AT A CALVARY NEAR THE ANCRE

One ever hangs where shelled roads part.
   In this war He too lost a limb,
But His disciples hide apart;
   And now the Soldiers bear with Him.

5 Near Golgotha strolls many a priest,
   And in their faces there is pride
That they were flesh-marked by the Beast
   By whom the gentle Christ's denied.

The scribes on all the people shove
10   And bawl allegiance to the state,
But they who love the greater love
   Lay down their life; they do not hate.

Written probably in late 1917 or early 1918, WO having been involved in
fighting near the river Ancre in January 1917 (CL, 421 n.). DH's note is to the
point: 'As in "The Parable of the Old Man and the Young", WO adapts
Biblical detail to fit the war. In the Gospel story, the *Soldiers* kept watch at
the cross while Christ's *disciples* hid in fear of the authorities; *priests* and *scribes*
passed by in scorn. The Church sends priests to the trenches, where they watch
the common soldier being, as it were, crucified, and they take pride in minor
wounds (*flesh-marked*, l. 7) as a sign of their opposition to Germany (*the Beast*).
Flesh-marked, however, carries a further meaning: the Devil used to be believed
to leave his finger-marks on the flesh of his followers (cf. Revelation 14: 9–10).
Thus the Church's hatred of Germany (l. 12) puts it in the Devil's following;
and the priests' wounds are signs not so much of opposition to the Devil
Germany as of allegiance to the Devil War. Christ said "Love one another" *and*
"Love your enemies"; despite the exhortations of Church and State, WO
perceives that "pure Christianity will not fit in with pure patriotism" [CL, 461].'
(DH, 116)

TITLE Calvary or Golgotha (both words meaning 'the place of the skull', from
       Lat. *calvaria* and Heb. *gulgōleth* respectively) was the site of the
       Crucifixion. A Calvary is a model of the crucified Christ, such as is found
       at many crossroads in France.

    4 Two senses of 'bear with' seem intended: 'humour' and 'carry the cross with'.

11–12 John 15: 13: 'Greater love hath no man than this, that a man lay down
       his life for his friends.' See also 'Greater Love' (p. 143).

CP&F, 287

MINERS

There was a whispering in my hearth,
    A sigh of the coal,
Grown wistful of a former earth
    It might recall.

5   I listened for a tale of leaves
    And smothered ferns,
Frond-forests, and the low sly lives
    Before the fauns.

My fire might show steam-phantoms simmer
10   From Time's old cauldron,
Before the birds made nests in summer,
    Or men had children.

But the coals were murmuring of their mine,
    And moans down there
15   Of boys that slept wry sleep, and men
    Writhing for air.

And I saw white bones in the cinder-shard,
    Bones without number.
Many the muscled bodies charred,
20   And few remember.

I thought of all that worked dark pits
    Of war, and died
Digging the rock where Death reputes
    Peace lies indeed.

25   Comforted years will sit soft-chaired,
    In rooms of amber;
The years will stretch their hands, well-cheered
    By our life's ember;

The centuries will burn rich loads
30   With which we groaned,
Whose warmth shall lull their dreaming lids,

While songs are crooned;
But they will not dream of us poor lads,
    Left in the ground.

Written at Scarborough on 13 or 14 January 1918 (WO, 253–7). On 12 January a pit explosion at the Podmore Hall Colliery, Halmerend, killed about 140 men and boy miners. WO presumably read the newspaper accounts, that in the *Daily News* of 14 January being headlined 'Colliery Disaster', and the same day he told SO: 'Wrote a poem on the Colliery Disaster: but I get mixed up with the War at the end. It is short, but oh! sour.' (EB, 125) He showed it to SS, who proposed alterations which, with questionable judgement, WO would seem to have accepted (see CP&F, 287). On 17 January he sent his mother 'the Coal Poem' and two days later wrote to her: 'With your beautiful letter came a proof from the *Nation* of my "Miners". This is the first poem I have sent to the *Nation* myself, and it has evidently been accepted. It was scrawled out on the back of a note to the Editor; and no penny stamp or addressed envelope was enclosed for return! That's the way to do it. "Miners" will probably appear next Saturday [26 January].' It did, and that evening WO wrote to ELG: 'You may feel keen enough to buy this week's *Nation*. I have at last a poem in it, which I sent off on the same evening as writing!!.' This produced 'blunt criticism' from ELG, whose 'musical ear' was offended by his cousin's rhymes, and on 12 February WO replied: 'I suppose I am doing in poetry what the advanced composers are doing in music. I am not satisfied with either. Still I am satisfied with the <u>Two</u> Guineas that half-hour's work brought me. Got the Cheque this m'ng!' (CL, 527–31)

DH ('Wilfred Owen and the Georgians', RES, n.s., xxx, no. 117 [1979], 28–40) has detected the influence of the introductory poem in W. W. Gibson's *Fires* (1912). Gibson sees pleasant pictures in the embers, including forests:

    Till, dazzled by the drowsy glare,
    I shut my eyes to heat and light;
    And saw, in sudden night,
    Crouched in the dripping dark,
    With steaming shoulders stark,
    The man who hews the coal to feed my fire.

In 'Miners', the watcher by the hearth expects the coal to tell of its prehistoric origin – WO was an amateur geologist – but instead it speaks of the sufferings of miners, in whom WO had been interested (WO, 76–8, 136–7, 230) long before he commanded a platoon containing several in 1916. The Halmerend disaster prompts a vision of the fate of such miners and those others who dug perilous 'saps' under No Man's Land to mine the enemy lines. At the poem's end WO sees himself sharing their common trench, mine, grave, hell. See Jennifer Breen, 'The Dating and Sources of Wilfred Owen's "Miners"', N&Q, n.s., xxi, no. 10 (October 1974), 366–70, and William Cooke, 'Wilfred Owen's "Miners" and the Minnie Pit Disaster', *English*, xxvi, no. 126 (Autumn 1977), 213–17.

    8 fauns (WO wrote 'fawns'): Cp. 'Sweet is your antique body, not yet young' (p. 106), l. 8.

THE LETTER

With B.E.F. June 10. Dear Wife,
(Oh blast this pencil. 'Ere, Bill, lend's a knife.)
I'm in the pink at present, dear.
I think the war will end this year.
5   We don't see much of them square-'eaded 'Uns.
We're out of harm's way, not bad fed.
I'm longing for a taste of your old buns.
(Say, Jimmie, spare's a bite of bread.)
There don't seem much to say just now.
10   (Yer what? Then don't, yer ruddy cow!
And give us back me cigarette!)
I'll soon be 'ome. You mustn't fret.
My feet's improvin', as I told you of.
We're out in rest now. Never fear.
15   (VRACH! By crumbs, but that was near.)
Mother might spare you half a sov.
Kiss Nell and Bert. When me and you –
(Eh? What the 'ell! Stand to? Stand to!
Jim, give's a hand with pack on, lad.
20   Guh! Christ! I'm hit. Take 'old. Aye, bad.
No, damn your iodine. Jim? 'Ere!
Write my old girl, Jim, there's a dear.)

Written, probably at Scarborough but possibly at Ripon, between January and
March 1918.

    1 B.E.F.: British Expeditionary Force.
    3 in the pink: in very good health.
   18 Stand to: Abbreviated form of the command 'Stand to arms', meaning
       'Prepare for/to attack'.

CP&F, 288

---

   19 Previous editors read 'For many hearts with coal are charred', an
       interlinear suggestion added to the MS by SS. I prefer WO's original line.
   24 lies: A pun would be in keeping with the tone of the poem.
   34 Previous editors read 'Lost in the ground', an interlinear suggestion
       added to the MS by SS. I prefer WO's original verb.

CP&F, 287

CONSCIOUS

His fingers wake, and flutter; up the bed.
His eyes come open with a pull of will,
Helped by the yellow mayflowers by his head.
The blind-cord drawls across the window-sill . . .
5   What a smooth floor the ward has! What a rug!
Who is that talking somewhere out of sight?
Three flies are creeping round the shiny jug . . .
'Nurse! Doctor!' – 'Yes, all right, all right.'

But sudden evening blurs and fogs the air.
10 There seems no time to want a drink of water.
Nurse looks so far away. And here and there
Music and roses burst through crimson slaughter.
He can't remember where he saw blue sky . . .
The trench is narrower. Cold, he's cold; yet hot –
15 And there's no light to see the voices by . . .
There is no time to ask . . . he knows not what.

Written, probably at Scarborough but possibly at Ripon, between January and
March 1918, this poem shows the influence of SS, 'The Death-Bed' (WO, 256).

    3 Cp. WO to MO from 13th Casualty Clearing Station, 8 May 1917:
       'Meanwhile I have superb weather, sociably-possible friends, great blue
       bowls of yellow Mayflower, baths and bed *ad lib*' (CL, 456).
    9 Cp. WO to SO, 14 August 1912: 'sudden twilight seemed to fall upon the
       world' (CL, 153).
  10 Cp. SS, 'The Death-Bed', l. 7: 'Someone was holding water to his mouth.'
  12 Cp. SS, 'The Death-Bed', l. 9: 'Through crimson gloom to darkness'.

CP&F, 288

SCHOOLMISTRESS

Having, with bold Horatius, stamped her feet
And waved a final swashing arabesque
O'er the brave days of old, she ceased to bleat,
Slapped her Macaulay back upon the desk,
5   Resumed her calm gaze and her lofty seat.

There, while she heard the classic lines repeat,
Once more the teacher's face clenched stern;
For through the window, looking on the street,
Three soldiers hailed her. She made no return.
10   One was called 'Orace whom she would not greet.

Written, probably at Scarborough but possibly at Ripon, between January and
March 1918, this poem may derive from WO's experience at the Tynecastle
Secondary School, Edinburgh, where he gave English lessons in
September–October 1917 (WO, 215).

TITLE EB and CDL entitle this poem 'Bold Horatius'.
    1 The schoolmistress has been reading Thomas Babington Macaulay's
        poem 'Horatius' from *Lays of Ancient Rome*.

CP&F, 290

DULCE ET DECORUM EST

Bent double, like old beggars under sacks,
Knock-kneed, coughing like hags, we cursed through sludge,
Till on the haunting flares we turned our backs
And towards our distant rest began to trudge.
5 Men marched asleep. Many had lost their boots
But limped on, blood-shod. All went lame; all blind;
Drunk with fatigue; deaf even to the hoots
Of tired, outstripped Five-Nines that dropped behind.

Gas! GAS! Quick, boys! – An ecstasy of fumbling,
10 Fitting the clumsy helmets just in time;
But someone still was yelling out and stumbling,
And flound'ring like a man in fire or lime . . .
Dim, through the misty panes and thick green light,
As under a green sea, I saw him drowning.

15 In all my dreams, before my helpless sight,
He plunges at me, guttering, choking, drowning.

If in some smothering dreams you too could pace
Behind the wagon that we flung him in,
And watch the white eyes writhing in his face,
20 His hanging face, like a devil's sick of sin;
If you could hear, at every jolt, the blood
Come gargling from the froth-corrupted lungs,
Obscene as cancer, bitter as the cud
Of vile, incurable sores on innocent tongues, –
25 My friend, you would not tell with such high zest
To children ardent for some desperate glory,
The old Lie: Dulce et decorum est
Pro patria mori.

Drafted at Craiglockhart in the first half of October 1917 (WO, 226–8), this poem
was revised, probably at Scarborough but possibly at Ripon, between January
and March 1918. The earliest surviving MS is dated 'Oct. 8. 1917', and on the
[? 16th] WO wrote to SO: 'Here is a gas poem, done yesterday, (which is not
private, but not final). The famous Latin tag [from Horace, *Odes*, III. ii. 13]

means of course It is sweet and meet to die for one's country. Sweet! and decorous!' (CL, 499–500)

5 Men . . . Many: Cp. WO to SO, 16 January 1917: '. . . craters full of water. Men have been known to drown in them. Many stuck in the mud . . .' (CL, 427)

8 WO never finalized this line (see MS on CP&F, 292). Five-Nines: 5.9-calibre shells.

9 GAS: Cp. WO to SO, 19 January 1917: 'I went on ahead to scout – foolishly alone – and when, half a mile away from the party, got overtaken by GAS' (CL, 428).

12 flound'ring: 'I remember [WO] using this word floundering and, unable to resist the play, adding, " . . . but of course there is, I suppose, the possibility you might founder" ' (JFO, III. 132).

13 panes: The gas mask's celluloid windows.

17–25 you . . . My friend: Jessie Pope, to whom the poem was originally to have been dedicated, was the author of numerous pre-war children's books, as well as of *Jessie Pope's War Poems* (1915), *More War Poems* (1915), and *Simple Rhymes for Stirring Times* (1916) (WO, 227).

CP&F, 292

A TEAR SONG

Out of the endless nave
    Chorus tremendous,
While the gruff organ gave
    Sponses stupendous.

5   But of a surety
    Not one among them
Said the psalms heartfully
    Of all that sung them,

Saving one chorister,
10   Sweet as gay bugles when
Robin the Forester
    Rallied his merry men.

Opened his little teeth
    Like the round daisy's.
15   Smiled they for things beneath,
    Or Zion's praises?

He sang of friendly bees
    Not of the hills that skip,
It was that morning's breeze
20   Piped on his lip.

But his eyes jewelled were
    Of his own singing,
God saw the sparkle there
    On his lids clinging.

25   God the boy's jewel took
    Into His casket,
Flinging the anthem book
    On His waste-basket.

God for his glittering world
30   Seeketh our tears.
Prayers show as eyelids pearled.
        God hath no ears.

Drafted, probably at Scarborough, between November 1917 and January 1918, and revised between January and March.

    25–6 Cp. Keats, 'Isabella', liv: 'So that the jewel, safely casketed, / Came
        forth'.

CP&F, 298

THE DEAD-BEAT

He dropped, – more sullenly than wearily,
Lay stupid like a cod, heavy like meat,
And none of us could kick him to his feet;
– Just blinked at my revolver, blearily;
5 – Didn't appear to know a war was on,
Or see the blasted trench at which he stared.
'I'll do 'em in,' he whined. 'If this hand's spared,
I'll murder them, I will.'

          A low voice said,
'It's Blighty, p'raps, he sees; his pluck's all gone,
10 Dreaming of all the valiant, that *aren't* dead:
Bold uncles, smiling ministerially;
Maybe his brave young wife, getting her fun
In some new home, improved materially.
It's not these stiffs have crazed him; nor the Hun.'

15 We sent him down at last, out of the way.
Unwounded; – stout lad, too, before that strafe.
Malingering? Stretcher-bearers winked, 'Not half!'

Next day I heard the Doc's well-whiskied laugh:
'That scum you sent last night soon died. Hooray!'

Begun on 22 August 1917, when WO wrote to ELG: 'At last I have an event
worth a letter. I have beknown myself to Siegfried Sassoon. Went in to him last
night (my second call). . . . After leaving him, I wrote something in Sassoon's
style, which I may as well send you, since you ask for the latest.' A fair copy of
'The Dead-Beat' followed, and the next day WO continued his letter: '. . . He
was struck with the "Dead Beat", but pointed out that the facetious bit was out
of keeping with the first & last stanzas. Thus the piece as a whole is no good.'
(CL, 485–6) WO salvaged – and probably adapted – eight lines of 'the facetious
bit' for his editorial in *The Hydra*, no. 10 (1 September 1917). The poem was
revised at Ripon between March and May 1918.

    9 Blighty: soldiers' slang for 'Britain'.
    16 strafe: artillery bombardment (from the German phrase, *Gott strafe
       England*, meaning 'God punish England').

CP&F, 298

INSENSIBILITY

1

Happy are men who yet before they are killed
Can let their veins run cold.
Whom no compassion fleers
Or makes their feet
5 Sore on the alleys cobbled with their brothers.
The front line withers.
But they are troops who fade, not flowers,
For poets' tearful fooling:
Men, gaps for filling:
10 Losses, who might have fought
Longer; but no one bothers.

2

And some cease feeling
Even themselves or for themselves.
Dullness best solves
15 The tease and doubt of shelling,
And Chance's strange arithmetic
Comes simpler than the reckoning of their shilling.
They keep no check on armies' decimation.

3

Happy are these who lose imagination:
20 They have enough to carry with ammunition.
Their spirit drags no pack.
Their old wounds, save with cold, can not more ache.
Having seen all things red,
Their eyes are rid
25 Of the hurt of the colour of blood for ever.
And terror's first constriction over,
Their hearts remain small-drawn.
Their senses in some scorching cautery of battle
Now long since ironed,
30 Can laugh among the dying, unconcerned.

4

Happy the soldier home, with not a notion
How somewhere, every dawn, some men attack,
And many sighs are drained.
Happy the lad whose mind was never trained:
35   His days are worth forgetting more than not.
He sings along the march
Which we march taciturn, because of dusk,
The long, forlorn, relentless trend
From larger day to huger night.

5

40   We wise, who with a thought besmirch
Blood over all our soul,
How should we see our task
But through his blunt and lashless eyes?
Alive, he is not vital overmuch;
45   Dying, not mortal overmuch;
Nor sad, nor proud,
Nor curious at all.
He cannot tell
Old men's placidity from his.

6

50   But cursed are dullards whom no cannon stuns,
That they should be as stones.
Wretched are they, and mean
With paucity that never was simplicity.
By choice they made themselves immune
55   To pity and whatever moans in man
Before the last sea and the hapless stars;
Whatever mourns when many leave these shores;
Whatever shares
The eternal reciprocity of tears.

Drafted either at Craiglockhart in October–November 1917, or at Scarborough
between November 1917 and January 1918, this Pindaric ode – perhaps a reply
to Wordsworth's 'Character of the Happy Warrior' (WO, 261) – may have been
revised at Ripon in April 1918. WO wrote to ELG on 21 April: 'In my

Chaumbers under the roof of a cottage (7 Borage Lane, Ripon) I have written, I think, two poems: one an Ode which, considering my tuneless tendencies, may be called dam good, excuse me' (CL, 546–7). However, DH argues persuasively (in a letter to the editor) that WO is here referring to his 'Elegy in April and September' (No. 173), which in its April version was entitled 'Ode for a Poet' and given musical annotations (see p. 184).

TITLE   Cp. Shelley, 'A Defence of Poetry': 'It [Poetry] is as it were the interpenetration of a diviner nature through our own; but its footsteps are like those of a wind over a sea, which the coming calm erases, and those traces remain only, as on the wrinkled sand which paves it. These and corresponding conditions of being are experienced principally by those of the most delicate sensibility and the most enlarged imagination; and the state of mind produced by them is at war with every base desire.'

1   Cp. Wordsworth, 'Character of the Happy Warrior', ll. 1–2: 'Who is the happy Warrior? Who is he / That every man in arms should wish to be?'

5   cobbled with their brothers: Cp. WO to MO, ? 25 March 1918: 'They are dying again at Beaumont Hamel, which already in 1916 was cobbled with skulls' (CL, 542).

8   fooling: Cp. 'Six O'clock in Princes Street' (p. 79), l. 5: 'Neither should I go fooling over clouds.'

9   gaps for filling: DH notes that 'The gaps had been illustrated on a number of recruiting posters. "Fill up the Ranks!" was a familiar slogan; one poster shows a long line of men in which a single empty space is filled by a billboard marked "This space is Reserved for a Fit Man". The repeated use of the word "happy" in the . . . poem, to describe the soldier who has been rendered "insensible to war" by war experience, is reminiscent of another poster which shows a smiling Tommy and the caption, "He's happy and satisfied / Are You?".' ('Some Contemporary Allusions in Poems by Rosenberg, Owen and Sassoon', N&Q, n.s., xxvi, no. 4 [August 1979], 333)

17   shilling: The 'King's shilling' was that traditionally given to the newly enlisted soldier by the recruiting officer.

19   imagination: Cp. Shelley, 'A Defence of Poetry', quoted above.

40   We wise: we poets.

55   moans: SS, CDL, and DH (but see DH, 125) read 'mourns'. WO, however, clearly cancelled 'mourns' and wrote 'moans' above it. See p. 301

56   Cp. Tennyson, 'Oenone', l. 215: 'Between the loud stream and the trembling stars'.

59   reciprocity: Cp. John Drinkwater, 'Reciprocity', a poem printed in *The Hydra*, New Series, no. 1, 2. There is a MS among WO's papers.

CP&F, 301

STRANGE MEETING

It seemed that out of battle I escaped
Down some profound dull tunnel, long since scooped
Through granites which titanic wars had groined.

Yet also there encumbered sleepers groaned,
5   Too fast in thought or death to be bestirred.
Then, as I probed them, one sprang up, and stared
With piteous recognition in fixed eyes,
Lifting distressful hands, as if to bless.
And by his smile, I knew that sullen hall, –
10 By his dead smile I knew we stood in Hell.

With a thousand pains that vision's face was grained;
Yet no blood reached there from the upper ground,
And no guns thumped, or down the flues made moan.
'Strange friend,' I said, 'here is no cause to mourn.'
15 'None,' said that other, 'save the undone years,
The hopelessness. Whatever hope is yours,
Was my life also; I went hunting wild
After the wildest beauty in the world,
Which lies not calm in eyes, or braided hair,
20 But mocks the steady running of the hour,
And if it grieves, grieves richlier than here.
For by my glee might many men have laughed,
And of my weeping something had been left,
Which must die now. I mean the truth untold,
25 The pity of war, the pity war distilled.
Now men will go content with what we spoiled,
Or, discontent, boil bloody, and be spilled.
They will be swift with swiftness of the tigress.
None will break ranks, though nations trek from progress.
30   Courage was mine, and I had mystery,
Wisdom was mine, and I had mastery:
To miss the march of this retreating world
Into vain citadels that are not walled.
Then, when much blood had clogged their chariot-wheels,
35 I would go up and wash them from sweet wells,
Even with truths that lie too deep for taint.

I would have poured my spirit without stint
But not through wounds; not on the cess of war.
Foreheads of men have bled where no wounds were.

40 'I am the enemy you killed, my friend.
I knew you in this dark: for so you frowned
Yesterday through me as you jabbed and killed.
I parried; but my hands were loath and cold.
Let us sleep now. . . .'

Drafted, probably at Scarborough but possibly at Ripon, between January
and March 1918, this poem may be a development of the fragment, 'With
those that are become' (CP&F, 492), drafted in November 1917. Certainly, it
incorporates another fragment, 'Earth's wheels run oiled with blood' (CP&F, 514),
written between November 1917 and January 1918. For a full and illuminating
discussion of the interplay of echoes in 'Strange Meeting' from the Bible,
Barbusse, Cary's translation of Dante, Keats, Shelley, Sir Lewis Morris,
Harold Monro, and SS, see Bäckman, 96–117. The MSS suggest that WO may
not have regarded the poem as complete.

TITLE   Welland was the first to cp. Shelley, *The Revolt of Islam*, ll. 1828–32:
                And one whose spear had pierced me, leaned beside,
                    With quivering lips and humid eyes; – and all
                Seemed like some brothers on a journey wide
                    Gone forth, whom now strange meeting did befall
                    In a strange land. . . .
            Cp. also Harold Monro, *Strange Meetings* (1917).
      2   tunnel: Cp. SS, 'The Rear-Guard', ll. 1–3:
                Groping along the tunnel, step by step,
                He winked his prying torch with patching glare
                From side to side, and sniffed the unwholesome air.
            Bäckman suggests the influence of a childhood memory of a nightmare
            walk down an 'immensely long and dark' drive, roofed with trees 'so that
            the effect was of a rather dark tunnel' (JFO, I. 80).
            scooped: Cp. Shelley, *The Revolt of Islam*, ll. 2913–15:
                He plunged through the green silence of the main,
                    Through many a cavern which the eternal flood
                    Had scooped, as dark lairs for its monster brood. . . .
            Also *Alastor*, ll. 423–5:
                                        There, huge caves,
                Scooped in the dark base of their aëry rocks
                Mocking its moans, respond and roar for ever.
      3   granites: Cp. WO to SO, 18 ? February 1917: 'the men had to dig
            trenches in ground like granite' (CL, 436).

4 encumbered: Cp. WO to SO, 1 February 1916: 'When I was going up the subway at Liverpool St. from the Underground to the Gt. Eastern Platform, I noticed the passages unduly encumbered, and found the outlet just closed' (CL, 377).

6–11 Cp. the poet's vision of Moneta's face, 'bright-blanched / By an immortal sickness which kills not' in Keats, 'The Fall of Hyperion'; also Dante, *Hell* (in the 1805 translation by the Revd Henry Francis Cary, a copy of which WO possessed), XV. 22–9:

> I was agnized of one, who by the skirt
> Caught me, and cried, 'What wonder have we here?'
> And I, when he to me outstretch'd his arm,
>   Intently fix'd my ken on his parch'd looks,
> That, although smirch'd with fire, they hinder'd not
> But I remember'd him; and towards his face
>   My hand inclining, answer'd, 'Ser Brunetto!
> And are ye here?'

25 Cp. WO's Preface (p. 192): 'My subject is War, and the pity of War. The Poetry is in the pity.'

28 Cp. II Samuel 1: 23: 'Saul and Jonathan were lovely and pleasant in their lives, and in their death they were not divided: they were swifter than eagles, they were stronger than lions.'

29 Presumably an allusion to the Great Trek of the South African Boer farmers in 1835–6.

32 Cp. 'The Fates' (p. 64), l. 14: 'And miss the march of lifetime, stage by stage.'

34 chariot-wheels: Cp. Shelley, *Queen Mab*, VII. 33–5:
>   whether hosts
> Stain his death-blushing chariot-wheels, as on
> Triumphantly they roll, ...

36 Cp. Wordsworth, Ode on 'Intimations of Immortality from Recollections of Early Childhood', l. 205: 'Thoughts that do often lie too deep for tears'.

39 Cp. Luke 22: 44: 'and his sweat was as it were great drops of blood falling to the ground.'

40 Cp. Oscar Wilde, 'The Ballad of Reading Gaol', l. 37: 'Yet each man kills the thing he loves.' This line, misquoted, appears in the fragment, 'With those that are become' (CP&F, 492). Cp. also Henri Barbusse, *Under Fire* (1917), 288: 'When I'm sleeping I dream that I'm killing him over again!'

44 Cp. 'Science has looked and sees no life but this' (p. 15): 'Let me but sleep . . .', and the fragment, 'The Women and the Slain' (CP&F, 502): 'Keep silent. Let us sleep' (line cancelled).

CP&F, 306

SONNET

On Seeing a Piece of Our Heavy Artillery
Brought into Action

Be slowly lifted up, thou long black arm,
Great Gun towering towards Heaven, about to curse;
Sway steep against them, and for years rehearse
Huge imprecations like a blasting charm!
5   Reach at that Arrogance which needs thy harm,
And beat it down before its sins grow worse.
Spend our resentment, cannon, – yea, disburse
Our gold in shapes of flame, our breaths in storm.

Yet, for men's sakes whom thy vast malison
10   Must wither innocent of enmity,
Be not withdrawn, dark arm, thy spoilure done,
Safe to the bosom of our prosperity.
But when thy spell be cast complete and whole,
May God curse thee, and cut thee from our soul!

Revised at Scarborough in May 1918, but perhaps begun as early as July 1917.

9 malison: malediction, curse.

CP&F, 311

[128]

ASLEEP

Under his helmet, up against his pack,
After so many days of work and waking,
Sleep took him by the brow and laid him back.

There, in the happy no-time of his sleeping,
5   Death took him by the heart. There heaved a quaking
Of the aborted life within him leaping,
Then chest and sleepy arms once more fell slack.

And soon the slow, stray blood came creeping
From the intruding lead, like ants on track.

10 Whether his deeper sleep lie shaded by the shaking
Of great wings, and the thoughts that hung the stars,
High-pillowed on calm pillows of God's making,
Above these clouds, these rains, these sleets of lead,
And these winds' scimitars,
15 – Or whether yet his thin and sodden head
Confuses more and more with the low mould,
His hair being one with the grey grass
Of finished fields, and wire-scrags rusty-old,
Who knows? Who hopes? Who troubles? Let it pass!
20 He sleeps. He sleeps less tremulous, less cold,
Than we who wake, and waking say Alas!

Written, probably in Shrewsbury, on 14 November 1917 (WO, 237–**8**) and
revised at Ripon the following May. On 16 November 1917, WO wrote to ELG:
'Good of you to send me the Lyric of Nov. 14th. I can only send my own of the
same date, which came from Winchester Downs, as I crossed the long backs of
the downs after leaving you. It is written <u>as from</u> the trenches. I could almost see
the dead lying about in the hollows of the downs.' (CL, 508) The subject of the
poem suggests an acquaintance with Rimbaud's 'Le dormeur du val'. DH
argues persuasively for the influence of Robert Graves's *Fairies and Fusiliers*
(1917), which WO bought on the day he began 'Asleep' ('Wilfred Owen and the

Georgians', RES, n.s., XXX, no. 117 [1979], 36); and Bäckman detects and discusses (40–2) an important debt to Milton's 'Lycidas'. Previous editors follow an earlier version.

1–9 Cp. Swinburne, 'Laus Veneris', ll. 1–4:
    Asleep or waking is it? for her neck,
    Kissed over close, wears yet a purple speck
       Wherein the pained blood falters and goes out;
    Soft, and stung softly – fairer for a fleck.

17 Cp. WO to SO, 24 May 1914: 'It was curious you asked about my grey hairs, for just last week I noticed they were cropping up again. In winter they died down, with the grass.' (CL, 252)

CP&F, 312

ARMS AND THE BOY

Let the boy try along this bayonet-blade
How cold steel is, and keen with hunger of blood;
Blue with all malice, like a madman's flash;
And thinly drawn with famishing for flesh.

5 Lend him to stroke these blind, blunt bullet-leads,
Which long to nuzzle in the hearts of lads,
Or give him cartridges whose fine zinc teeth
Are sharp with sharpness of grief and death.

For his teeth seem for laughing round an apple.
10 There lurk no claws behind his fingers supple;
And God will grow no talons at his heels,
Nor antlers through the thickness of his curls.

Written, or at any rate fair-copied, at 7 Borrage Lane, Ripon, on 3 May 1918,
this poem was classified by WO in his draft list of contents (Appendix B) under
'Protest – the unnaturalness of weapons'.

TITLE Cp. SS, 'Arms and the Man' and Harold Monro, 'Youth in Arms'.

  1–4 Cp. Shelley, *The Mask of Anarchy*, lxxvii. ll. 311–14:
> Let the fixèd bayonet
> Gleam with sharp desire to wet
> Its bright point in English blood
> Looking keen as one for food.

    6 Paul Fussell observes that 'Bret Harte's "What the Bullet Sang", one of
the few American poems available in the *Oxford Book* [*of English Verse*,
edited by Sir Arthur Quiller-Couch], seems to lie behind both Sassoon's
"The Kiss" and Owen's "Arms and the Boy", both of which, like Harte's
poem, make much of the quasi-erotic desire of the bullet (and in
Sassoon, the bayonet) to "kiss" or "nuzzle" the body of its adolescent
target.' (*The Great War and Modern Memory* [1975], 160)

CP&F, 315

THE SHOW

We have fallen in the dreams the ever-living
Breathe on the tarnished mirror of the world,
And then smooth out with ivory hands and sigh.

W. B. YEATS

My soul looked down from a vague height, with Death,
As unremembering how I rose or why,
And saw a sad land, weak with sweats of dearth,
Grey, cratered like the moon with hollow woe,
5   And pitted with great pocks and scabs of plagues.

Across its beard, that horror of harsh wire,
There moved thin caterpillars, slowly uncoiled.
It seemed they pushed themselves to be as plugs
Of ditches, where they writhed and shrivelled, killed.

10 By them had slimy paths been trailed and scraped
Round myriad warts that might be little hills.

From gloom's last dregs these long-strung creatures crept,
And vanished out of dawn down hidden holes.

(And smell came up from those foul openings
15 As out of mouths, or deep wounds deepening.)

On dithering feet upgathered, more and more,
Brown strings, towards strings of grey, with bristling spines,
All migrants from green fields, intent on mire.

Those that were grey, of more abundant spawns,
20 Ramped on the rest and ate them and were eaten.

I saw their bitten backs curve, loop, and straighten.
I watched those agonies curl, lift, and flatten.

Whereat, in terror what that sight might mean,
I reeled and shivered earthward like a feather.

25　And Death fell with me, like a deepening moan.
And He, picking a manner of worm, which half had hid
Its bruises in the earth, but crawled no further,
Showed me its feet, the feet of many men,
And the fresh-severed head of it, my head.

Drafted at Scarborough in November 1917 and revised at Ripon in May 1918
(WO, **243**–5), this is almost certainly the poem referred to in WO to SS, 27
November 1917: 'My "Vision" is the result of two hours' leisure yesterday, –
and getting up early this morning! If you have objections to make, would you
return it? If not, pass it on to R[obbie]. R[oss].' (CL, 512) That this 'Vision' was
what came to be called 'The Show' (and not the fragment [CP&F, 481] 'A
Vision in Whitechapel', later retitled 'Lines to a Beauty seen in Limehouse', as
the editors of CL suggest) is made clear by WO to SS of 6 December 1917:
'What do you think of my Vowel-rime stunt in this ['Wild with all Regrets', to
become 'A Terre' (p. 155)], and "Vision"?' (CL, 514)
　　WO's vision derives from his experience of battlefields between January and
May 1917 (see notes to ll. 5 and 26–7 below) and from his reading in
November–December 1917 of Henri Barbusse, *Under Fire* (1917). Chapter i of
this is entitled 'The Vision':
　　'The man at the end of the rank cries, "I can see crawling things down there"
– "Yes, as though they were alive" – "Some sort of plant perhaps" – "Some
kind of men" –
　　'And there amid the baleful glimmers of the storm, below the dark disorder of
the clouds that extend and unfurl over the earth like evil spirits, they seem to see
a great livid plain unrolled, which to their seeing is made of mud and water,
while figures appear and fast fix themselves to the surface of it, all blinded and
borne down with filth, like the dreadful castaways of shipwreck.' (4)
　　'The Show' may also echo two passages from chapter xx: 'Dwarfed to the size
of insects and worms, they make a queer dark stirring among these
shadow-hidden and Death-pacified lands . . . (255); and 'In the middle of the
plateau and in the depth of the rainy and bitter air, on the ghastly morrow of this
debauch of slaughter, there is a head planted in the ground, a wet and bloodless
head, with a heavy beard. It is one of ours, and the helmet is beside it.' (265)

TITLE 'Show' was soldiers' slang for 'battle'. Cp. 'The Chances' (p. 148) l. 1:
　　　'the night before that show'.
EPIGRAPH WO misquotes Forgael's speech in Yeats's play *The Shadowy
　　　Waters (Poems 1899–1905* [1906], 22), which reads 'burnished
　　　mirror' (WO, 245). (For WO's ironic use of Yeatsian epigraphs,
　　　see Jon Stallworthy, 'W. B. Yeats and Wilfred Owen', *Critical
　　　Quarterly*, xi, no. 3 [Autumn 1969], 199–214.)
　　4–5 Cp. WO to SO, 19 January 1917: '[No Man's Land] is pock-
　　　marked like a body of foulest disease and its odour is the

breath of cancer. . . . No Man's Land under snow is like the face of the moon chaotic, crater-ridden, uninhabitable, awful, the abode of madness.' (CL, 429)

16–17 The caterpillars 'with bristling spines' are files of soldiers: the Germans in grey uniforms, the British in khaki.

26–7 Cp. WO to CO, 14 May 1917: 'Then we were caught in a Tornado of Shells. The various "waves" were all broken up and we carried on like a crowd moving off a cricket-field. When I looked back and saw the ground all crawling and wormy with wounded bodies, I felt no horror at all but only an immense exultation at having got through the Barrage.' (CL, 458)

29 See the quotation from Barbusse, 265, above. As the commander of a platoon advancing in single file, WO would have been literally and figuratively its 'head'.

CP&F, 316

FUTILITY

Move him into the sun –
Gently its touch awoke him once,
At home, whispering of fields half-sown.
Always it woke him, even in France,
5   Until this morning and this snow.
If anything might rouse him now
The kind old sun will know.

Think how it wakes the seeds –
Woke once the clays of a cold star.
10   Are limbs, so dear achieved, are sides
Full-nerved, still warm, too hard to stir?
Was it for this the clay grew tall?
– O what made fatuous sunbeams toil
To break earth's sleep at all?

Written at Ripon in May 1918.

TITLE   Cp. Tennyson, *In Memoriam*, lvi, l. 25: 'O life as futile, then, as frail!' For
        a discussion of the influence of Tennyson's elegy on WO's, see DH,
        Wilfred Owen (Writers and Their Work, 1975), 32–3.
    3   half-sown: Previous editors read 'unsown'.
    7   old sun: Cp. Donne, 'The Sun Rising', l. 1: 'Busy old fool, unruly sun'.
  8–9   Cp. John Davidson, 'Thirty Bob a Week', ll. 71–2: 'A little sleeping seed,
        I woke – I did, indeed – / A million years before the blooming sun.' Also
        Sir Walter Scott, Hymn 487, *The English Hymnal*, ll. 9–12:
            O, on that day, that wrathful day,
            When man to judgement wakes from clay,
            Be thou the trembling sinner's stay,
            Though heaven and earth shall pass away!

CP&F, 319

THE END

After the blast of lightning from the east,
    The flourish of loud clouds, the Chariot Throne;
After the drums of time have rolled and ceased,
    And by the bronze west long retreat is blown,
5   Shall Life renew these bodies? Of a truth,
    All death will he annul, all tears assuage?
Or fill these void veins full again with youth,
    And wash, with an immortal water, age?

When I do ask white Age, he saith not so:
10   'My head hangs weighed with snow.'
And when I hearken to the Earth, she saith:
    'My fiery heart shrinks, aching. It is death.
Mine ancient scars shall not be glorified,
Nor my titanic tears, the seas, be dried.'

Begun probably in late 1916; continued either at Craiglockhart in
October–November 1917, or at Scarborough between November 1917 and
January 1918; this poem is almost certainly that referred to in WO's letter of 12
February 1917 to SO: 'Leslie tells me that Miss Joergens considers my Sonnet
on "The End" the finest of the lot. Naturally, because it is, intentionally, in her
style!' (CL, 434). 'To Eros' (p. 92), was also, at one time, entitled 'The End',
as was the unfinished fragment on CP&F, 491. ELG's 'The End' was
published in *YM / The British Empire YMCA Weekly*, ii, no. 102 (22 December
1916), 1229. DH discusses WO's poem's debt to Shelley, *Prometheus Unbound*
(*Wilfred Owen* [Writers and Their Work, 1975], 19–20), and Hilda D. Spear its
refutation of the biblical Book of Revelation ('"I Too Saw God": The Religious
Allusions in Wilfred Owen's Poetry', *English*, xxiv, no. 119 [Summer 1975],
35–6).

    5–6 Cp. Revelation 21:4, 'And God shall wipe away all tears from their eyes;
       and there shall be no more death, neither sorrow, nor crying.' For the
       misquotation from WO's lines on his tombstone, see WO, 288.
    14 titanic tears: Cp. 'Strange Meeting' (p. 125), l. 3: 'titanic wars'.

CP&F, 322

S. I. W.

> I will to the King,
> And offer him consolation in his trouble,
> For that man there has set his teeth to die,
> And being one that hates obedience,
> Discipline, and orderliness of life,
> I cannot mourn him.
>
> **W. B. YEATS**

I The Prologue

Patting goodbye, doubtless they told the lad
He'd always show the Hun a brave man's face;
Father would sooner him dead than in disgrace, –
Was proud to see him going, aye, and glad.
5 Perhaps his mother whimpered how she'd fret
Until he got a nice safe wound to nurse.
Sisters would wish girls too could shoot, charge, curse . . .
Brothers – would send his favourite cigarette.
Each week, month after month, they wrote the same,
10 Thinking him sheltered in some Y. M. Hut,
Because he said so, writing on his butt
Where once an hour a bullet missed its aim.
And misses teased the hunger of his brain.
His eyes grew old with wincing, and his hand
15 Reckless with ague. Courage leaked, as sand
From the best sandbags after years of rain.
But never leave, wound, fever, trench-foot, shock,
Untrapped the wretch. And death seemed still withheld
For torture of lying machinally shelled,
20 At the pleasure of this world's Powers who'd run amok.

He'd seen men shoot their hands, on night patrol.
Their people never knew. Yet they were vile.
'Death sooner than dishonour, that's the style!'
So Father said.

II The Action

One dawn, our wire patrol
25 Carried him. This time, Death had not missed.

We could do nothing but wipe his bleeding cough.
Could it be accident? – Rifles go off . . .
Not sniped? No. (Later they found the English ball.)

III   The Poem
It was the reasoned crisis of his soul
30   Against more days of inescapable thrall,
Against infrangibly wired and blind trench wall
Curtained with fire, roofed in with creeping fire,
Slow grazing fire, that would not burn him whole
But kept him for death's promises and scoff,
35   And life's half-promising, and both their riling.

IV   The Epilogue
With him they buried the muzzle his teeth had kissed,
And truthfully wrote the mother, 'Tim died smiling.'

Drafted at Craiglockhart in September 1917 and revised at Ripon in May 1918,
this poem shows the influence of such poems by SS as 'The Hero' and
'Stand-to: Good Friday Morning'.

TITLE   Military abbreviation for 'Self-Inflicted Wound'.

EPIGRAPH   From Yeats's play, *The King's Threshold*, *Poems 1899–1905* (1906),
238. (For WO's ironic use of Yeatsian epigraphs, see Jon Stallworthy,
'W. B. Yeats and Wilfred Owen', *Critical Quarterly*, xi, no. 3 [Autumn
1969], 199–214.)

10   Y. M. Hut: Young Men's Christian Association hostel.

31   blind trench: one with no outlet.

32   creeping fire: A 'creeping barrage' advanced a predetermined distance –
usually in front of advancing infantry – at a predetermined time.

CP&F, 327

THE CALLS

A dismal fog-hoarse siren howls at dawn.
I watch the man it calls for, pushed and drawn
Backwards and forwards, helpless as a pawn.
      But I'm lazy, and his work's crazy.

5   Quick treble bells begin at nine o'clock,
Scuttling the schoolboy pulling up his sock,
Scaring the late girl in the inky frock.
      I must be crazy; I learn from the daisy.

Stern bells annoy the rooks and doves at ten.
10   I watch the verger close the doors, and when
I hear the organ moan the first amen,
      Sing my religion's – same as pigeons'.

A blatant bugle tears my afternoons.
Out clump the clumsy Tommies by platoons,
15 Trying to keep in step with rag-time tunes,
      But I sit still; I've done my drill.

Gongs hum and buzz like saucepan-lids at dusk.
I see a food-hog whet his gold-filled tusk
To eat less bread, and more luxurious rusk.

20 Then sometimes late at night my window bumps
From gunnery-practice, till my small heart thumps
And listens for the shell-shrieks and the crumps,
      But that's not all.

For leaning out last midnight on my sill,
25 I heard the sighs of men, that have no skill
To speak of their distress, no, nor the will!
      A voice I know. And this time I must go.

Revised – it may have been written earlier – at Scarborough in May 1918 (WO, 266), and here treated as a poem rather than a fragment – although the manuscript makes clear that its revisions are incomplete – since it has gained

currency as such from its appearance in CDL and DH. On 10 August 1918, WO
wrote to SO: 'Tomorrow I am for a medical inspection with 21 others, to be
declared fit for draft. This means we may be sent on draft leave tomorrow, & I
may reach you even before this letter! I know not. I am glad. That is I am much
gladder to be going out again than afraid. I shall be better able to cry my outcry,
playing my part.' (CL, 568)

18–19 food-hog: Perhaps a reference to 'the stinking Leeds & Bradford
War-profiteers' mentioned in the letter to SO quoted above. DH notes
that '"Eat less bread" was a widespread slogan in the Food Economy
Campaign in 1917. One poster reads, "Save the Wheat / and / Help the
Fleet. / Eat / Less / Bread." The Food Controller sent a circular to
households in May 1917 and said, "We must all eat less food, especially
we must all eat less bread".' ('Some Contemporary Allusions in Poems
by Rosenberg, Owen and Sassoon', N&Q, n.s., xxvi, no. 4 [August 1979],
333–4)

19 The MS shows two cancelled attempts at a line following this, and one
must suppose that WO intended to try again.

23 Cancelled attempts at this line suggest that WO intended 'But that's not
all' to be only its second half.

CP&F, 332

TRAINING

Not this week nor this month dare I lie down
In languor under lime trees or smooth smile.
Love must not kiss my face pale that is brown.

My lips, panting, shall drink space, mile by mile;
5   Strong meats be all my hunger; my renown
Be the clean beauty of speed and pride of style.

Cold winds encountered on the racing Down
Shall thrill my heated bareness; but awhile
None else may meet me till I wear my crown.

Written, probably at Scarborough, in June 1918 (the date on the MS). WO
arrived in Scarborough, from Ripon, on 5 June and on 1 July 1918 wrote to SO:
'Went a Cross Country Run last Wednesday, from which my calves are still
suffering. Have seldom enjoyed any exercise so much.' (CL, 561)

    4 panting: EB and CDL read 'parting', which also fits the context, but is
      not, I think, what WO wrote.
    9 Cp. WO to OS, July 1918: 'For 14 hours yesterday I was at work –
      teaching Christ to lift his cross by numbers, and how to adjust his
      crown' (CL, 562).

CP&F, 334

THE NEXT WAR

> War's a joke for me and you,
> While we know such dreams are true.
> SIEGFRIED SASSOON

Out there, we walked quite friendly up to Death, –
   Sat down and ate beside him, cool and bland, –
   Pardoned his spilling mess-tins in our hand.
We've sniffed the green thick odour of his breath, –
5 Our eyes wept, but our courage didn't writhe.
   He's spat at us with bullets, and he's coughed
   Shrapnel. We chorused if he sang aloft,
We whistled while he shaved us with his scythe.

Oh, Death was never enemy of ours!
10 We laughed at him, we leagued with him, old chum.
No soldier's paid to kick against His powers.
   We laughed, – knowing that better men would come,
And greater wars: when every fighter brags
He fights on Death, for lives; not men, for flags.

Written at Craiglockhart in late September 1917 and sent, with 'Anthem for
Doomed Youth' (p. 76), to SO on the 25th (CL, 496). On 2 October 1917,
WO told her: 'I included my "Next War" in order to strike a note. I want Colin
to read, mark, learn etc. it.' (CL, 497) The poem was revised at Scarborough in
July 1918.

EPIGRAPH SS, 'A Letter Home' (to Robert Graves, written at Flixécourt in
     May 1916), ll. 73–4.
   14 on: against.

CP&F, 334

[142]

GREATER LOVE

Red lips are not so red
   As the stained stones kissed by the English dead.
Kindness of wooed and wooer
Seems shame to their love pure.
5 O Love, your eyes lose lure
   When I behold eyes blinded in my stead!

Your slender attitude
   Trembles not exquisite like limbs knife-skewed,
Rolling and rolling there
10 Where God seems not to care;
Till the fierce love they bear
   Cramps them in death's extreme decrepitude.

Your voice sings not so soft, –
   Though even as wind murmuring through raftered loft, –
15 Your dear voice is not dear,
Gentle, and evening clear,
As theirs whom none now hear,
   Now earth has stopped their piteous mouths that coughed.

Heart, you were never hot
20 Nor large, nor full like hearts made great with shot;
And though your hand be pale,
Paler are all which trail
Your cross through flame and hail:
   Weep, you may weep, for you may touch them not.

Drafted either at Craiglockhart in October–November 1917 (WO, 230–1), or at
Scarborough between November 1917 and January 1918, and revised at
Scarborough that July, the poem is a response to Swinburne's poem 'Before the
Mirror / (Verses Written under a Picture) / Inscribed to J. A. Whistler', ll. 1–7:
   White rose in red rose-garden
      Is not so white;
   Snowdrops that plead for pardon
      And pine for fright
   Because the hard East blows
   Over their maiden rows
      Grow not as this face grows from pale to bright.

WO may also have been aware of Salomé's words to Jokanaan in Wilde's *Salomé*: 'The roses in the garden of the Queen of Arabia are not so white as thy body.' WO had written to SO on 16 [?] May 1917: 'Christ is literally in no man's land. There men often hear His voice: Greater love hath no man than this, that a man lay down his life – for a friend.' (CL, 461)

TITLE   Cp. John 15:13: 'Greater love hath no man than this, that a man lay down his life for his friends.' See also 'At a Calvary near the Ancre' (p. 111), ll. 11–12: 'But they who love the greater love / Lay down their life; they do not hate.'

20   Cp. Elizabeth Barrett Browning, *Aurora Leigh*, Second Book, ll. 718–20:
                    As my blood recoiled
         From that imputed ignominy, I made
         My heart great with it.
     See also WO to SO, 2 April 1916: 'And the drums pulse fearfully-voluptuously, as great hearts in death' (CL, 388).

21   pale: Cp. Swinburne, 'Before the Mirror', quoted above.

22   trail: Used in the military sense of 'trail arms', carry a rifle with butt end near the ground and muzzle pointing forwards.

24   Cp. John 21:15–17: 'Jesus saith unto [Mary Magdalene], Woman, why weepest thou? . . . Jesus saith unto her, Touch me not; for I am not yet ascended to my Father.'

CP&F, 337

THE LAST LAUGH

'Oh! Jesus Christ! I'm hit,' he said; and died.
Whether he vainly cursed or prayed indeed,
      The Bullets chirped – In vain, vain, vain!
      Machine-guns chuckled – Tut-tut! Tut-tut!
5   And the Big Gun guffawed.

Another sighed – 'O Mother, – Mother, – Dad!'
Then smiled at nothing, childlike, being dead.
      And the lofty Shrapnel-cloud
      Leisurely gestured, – Fool!
10   And the splinters spat, and tittered.

'My Love!' one moaned. Love-languid seemed his mood,
Till slowly lowered, his whole face kissed the mud.
      And the Bayonets' long teeth grinned;
      Rabbles of Shells hooted and groaned;
15   And the Gas hissed.

Drafted at Scarborough in February 1918, an early version of this poem was
included in WO's letter of 18 February to SO, and was there prefaced: 'There
is a point where prayer is indistinguishable from blasphemy. There is also a
point where blasphemy is indistinguishable from prayer. As in this first verse . . .'
(CL, 534) The first of the three later drafts, in which full rhymes have given
place to pararhymes, is dated '5. 3. 18', and WO's subsequent revisions must
date from spring–summer 1918 when he gave a final fair copy to OS.

CP&F, 341

MENTAL CASES

Who are these? Why sit they here in twilight?
Wherefore rock they, purgatorial shadows,
Drooping tongues from jaws that slob their relish,
Baring teeth that leer like skulls' teeth wicked?
5   Stroke on stroke of pain, – but what slow panic,
Gouged these chasms round their fretted sockets?
Ever from their hair and through their hands' palms
Misery swelters. Surely we have perished
Sleeping, and walk hell; but who these hellish?

10   – These are men whose minds the Dead have ravished.
Memory fingers in their hair of murders,
Multitudinous murders they once witnessed.
Wading sloughs of flesh these helpless wander,
Treading blood from lungs that had loved laughter.
15   Always they must see these things and hear them,
Batter of guns and shatter of flying muscles,
Carnage incomparable, and human squander
Rucked too thick for these men's extrication.

Therefore still their eyeballs shrink tormented
20   Back into their brains, because on their sense
Sunlight seems a blood-smear; night comes blood-black;
Dawn breaks open like a wound that bleeds afresh.
– Thus their heads wear this hilarious, hideous,
Awful falseness of set-smiling corpses.
25   – Thus their hands are plucking at each other;
Picking at the rope-knouts of their scourging;
Snatching after us who smote them, brother,
Pawing us who dealt them war and madness.

Drafted at Ripon in May 1918 and revised at Scarborough in July, this poem
draws on the earlier fragment, 'Purgatorial Passions' (CP&F, 455). WO wrote
to SO on 25 May: 'I've been "busy" this evening with my terrific poem (at
present) called "The Deranged". This poem the Editor of the *Burlington
Magazine* – (a 2/6 Arts Journal which takes no poetry) – old More Adey, I say,
solemnly prohibited me from sending to the *English Review*, on the grounds that
"the *English Review* should not be encouraged".!!!!' (CL, 553) On 15 June 1918

he told SO: 'lo! an urgent request from the Sitwells in London for more of my poems for their 1918 Anthology which is coming out immediately. This is on the strength of "The Deranged", which S. Moncrieff showed them the other day.' (CL, 559) In the event, the Sitwells printed no poems by WO in their anthology *Wheels* (1918).

The poem reflects WO's reading of Dante, and Mr Mark Sinfield points out (in a letter to the editor) that the opening of each stanza echoes the diction and, with bitter irony, parallels the structure of the King James version of Revelation 7:13–17: 'What are these which are arrayed in white robes? and whence came they? . . . These are they which came out of great tribulation, and have washed their robes, and made them white in the blood of the Lamb. Therefore are they before the throne of God, and serve him day and night in his temple: and he that sitteth on the throne shall dwell among them. They shall hunger no more, neither thirst any more; neither shall the sun light on them, nor any heat. For the Lamb which is in the midst of the throne shall feed them, and shall lead them unto living fountains of waters: and God shall wipe away all tears from their eyes.'

12 Multitudinous murders: Cp. *Macbeth*, II. ii. 58–60:
> No; this my hand will rather
> The multitudinous seas incarnadine,
> Making the green one red.

19 The MS variants of this line confirm the impression that this poem owes something to the influence of Isaac Watts, 'The Day of Judgement', ll. 17–24:

> Hark, the shrill outcries of the guilty wretches!
> Lively bright horror, and amazing anguish,
> Stare thro' their eye-lids, while the living worm lies
> > Gnawing within them.
>
> Thoughts, like old vultures, prey upon their heart-strings,
> And the smart twinges, when the eye beholds the
> Lofty Judge frowning, and a flood of vengeance
> > Rolling afore him.

26 Cp. 'The Rime of the Youthful Mariner' (p. 108), ll. 1–3.

CP&F, 342

THE CHANCES

I 'mind as how the night before that show
Us five got talkin'; we was in the know.
'Ah well,' says Jimmy, and he's seen some scrappin',
'There ain't no more than five things as can happen, –
5   You get knocked out; else wounded, bad or cushy;
Scuppered; or nowt except you're feelin' mushy.'

One of us got the knock-out, blown to chops;
One lad was hurt, like, losin' both his props;
And one – to use the word of hypocrites –
10   Had the misfortune to be took by Fritz.
Now me, I wasn't scratched, praise God Almighty,
Though next time please I'll thank Him for a blighty.
But poor old Jim, he's livin' and he's not;
He reckoned he'd five chances, and he had:
15   He's wounded, killed, and pris'ner, all the lot,
The flamin' lot all rolled in one. Jim's mad.

Drafted at Craiglockhart in August–September 1917, this poem shows the
strong influence of SS. It was revised at Scarborough in July 1918.

    1 show: Soldiers' slang for 'battle'.
    2 Previous editors follow this line with a couplet omitted from the final
       version.
    5 cushy: Soldiers' slang for 'slightly'.
    6 scuppered: Soldiers' (from nautical) slang for 'killed'.
       nowt: Dialect for 'nothing'.
    8 props: Soldiers' slang for 'legs'.
    10 Fritz: Soldiers' slang for 'the Germans'.
    12 blighty: A wound serious enough to cause a soldier to be sent back to
        England.

CP&F, 345

THE SEND-OFF

Down the close darkening lanes they sang their way
To the siding-shed,
And lined the train with faces grimly gay.

Their breasts were stuck all white with wreath and spray
5   As men's are, dead.

Dull porters watched them, and a casual tramp
Stood staring hard,
Sorry to miss them from the upland camp.

Then, unmoved, signals nodded, and a lamp
10   Winked to the guard.

So secretly, like wrongs hushed-up, they went.
They were not ours:
We never heard to which front these were sent;

Nor there if they yet mock what women meant
15   Who gave them flowers.

Shall they return to beating of great bells
In wild train-loads?
A few, a few, too few for drums and yells,

May creep back, silent, to village wells,
20   Up half-known roads.

Drafted at Ripon in April–May 1918 (WO, 261–2), and revised at Scarborough
in July, this may be one of the 'two poems' mentioned in WO's letter to ELG of
21 April 1918 (CL, 547). On 4 May he was able to tell SO: 'I have long "waited"
for a final stanza to "the Draft" (which begins:

1

"Down the deep, darkening lanes they sang their way
To the waiting train,
And filled its doors with faces grimly gay,
And heads & shoulders white with wreath & spray,
As men's are, slain.")

* * * *

IV

Will they return, to beatings of great bells,
In wild train-loads?
– A few, a few, too few for drums and yells,
May walk back, silent, to their village wells,
Up half-known roads.'

(CL, 550)

6–8 Bäckman observes (43): 'These lines contain a couple of ironic echoes of
stanzas 25 and 27 of Gray's "Elegy", where a "hoary-headed swain" is
heard to say that he had often seen the departed country poet "brushing
with hasty steps the dews away, / To meet the sun upon *the upland lawn*",
but then suddenly "one morn", he "*miss'd* him on the custom'd hill". The
hoary-headed swain in Gray's lines about the death of an unknown poet
becomes "a casual tramp" in Owen's poem commemorating the departure
of some soldiers for the front, and Gray's poetic "upland lawn" becomes
the more prosaic "upland camp".'

19 Previous editors read 'still village wells'.

CP&F, 346

THE PARABLE OF THE OLD MAN AND THE YOUNG

So Abram rose, and clave the wood, and went,
And took the fire with him, and a knife.
And as they sojourned both of them together,
Isaac the first-born spake and said, My Father,
5   Behold the preparations, fire and iron,
But where the lamb, for this burnt-offering?
Then Abram bound the youth with belts and straps,
And builded parapets and trenches there,
And stretchèd forth the knife to slay his son.
10 When lo! an Angel called him out of heaven,
Saying, Lay not thy hand upon the lad,
Neither do anything to him, thy son.
Behold! Caught in a thicket by its horns,
A Ram. Offer the Ram of Pride instead.

15 But the old man would not so, but slew his son,
And half the seed of Europe, one by one.

Written, probably at Scarborough, in July 1918, the poem's ll. 1–14 follow the
wording of Genesis 22: 1–19 very closely.

    7 belts and straps: As of a soldier's equipment.
12–14 Previous editors print an earlier form of these lines.
    16 seed: Cp. '1914' (p. 93), l. 14: 'blood for seed'.

CP&F, 350

DISABLED

He sat in a wheeled chair, waiting for dark,
And shivered in his ghastly suit of grey,
Legless, sewn short at elbow. Through the park
Voices of boys rang saddening like a hymn,
5   Voices of play and pleasure after day,
Till gathering sleep had mothered them from him.

*   *   *

About this time Town used to swing so gay
When glow-lamps budded in the light blue trees,
And girls glanced lovelier as the air grew dim, –
10 In the old times, before he threw away his knees.
Now he will never feel again how slim
Girls' waists are, or how warm their subtle hands.
All of them touch him like some queer disease.

*   *   *

There was an artist silly for his face,
15 For it was younger than his youth, last year.
Now, he is old; his back will never brace;
He's lost his colour very far from here,
Poured it down shell-holes till the veins ran dry,
And half his lifetime lapsed in the hot race
20 And leap of purple spurted from his thigh.

*   *   *

One time he liked a blood-smear down his leg,
After the matches, carried shoulder-high.
It was after football, when he'd drunk a peg,
He thought he'd better join. – He wonders why.
25 Someone had said he'd look a god in kilts,
That's why; and maybe, too, to please his Meg,
Aye, that was it, to please the giddy jilts
He asked to join. He didn't have to beg;
Smiling they wrote his lie: aged nineteen years.

30   Germans he scarcely thought of; all their guilt,
     And Austria's, did not move him. And no fears
     Of Fear came yet. He thought of jewelled hilts
     For daggers in plaid socks; of smart salutes;
     And care of arms; and leave; and pay arrears;
35   Esprit de corps; and hints for young recruits.
     And soon, he was drafted out with drums and cheers.

*   *   *

Some cheered him home, but not as crowds cheer Goal.
Only a solemn man who brought him fruits
Thanked him; and then enquired about his soul.

*   *   *

40   Now, he will spend a few sick years in institutes,
     And do what things the rules consider wise,
     And take whatever pity they may dole.
     Tonight he noticed how the women's eyes
     Passed from him to the strong men that were whole.
45   How cold and late it is! Why don't they come
     And put him into bed? Why don't they come?

Drafted at Craiglockhart in October 1917 (WO, 224–6), and revised at
Scarborough in July 1918. On 14 October 1917 WO wrote to SO: 'On Sat. I
met Robert Graves. . . . No doubt he thought me a slacker sort of sub. S.S.
when they were together showed him my longish war-piece "Disabled" (you
haven't seen it) & it seems Graves was mightily impressed, and considers me a
kind of <u>Find</u>!! No thanks, Captain Graves! I'll find myself in due time.' (CL, 499)
On 18 October he told SO that Graves had 'carried away a Poem, or was
carried away with it, without my knowledge. It was only in a <u>Draft</u> State, & I was
perfectly aware of all the solecisms.' (CL, 501) A day or two earlier, Graves had
written to WO about that 'damn fine poem of yours, that "Disabled"' (CL, 595).

22 Cp. A. E. Housman, 'To an Athlete Dying Young', ll. 1–4:
     The time you won your town the race
     We chaired you through the market-place;
     Man and boy stood cheering by,
     And home we brought you shoulder-high.
23 peg: Slang expression for a drink, usually brandy and soda.
27 jilts: capricious women.

29   they wrote his lie: The recruiting officers entered on his enlistment form his lie that he was nineteen years old and therefore above the minimum age for military service.

45–6 DH calls attention to 'a mocking echo of the slogan on a recruiting poster, probably put out in 1914, which shows soldiers in action and in need of reinforcements. The slogan reads, "Will they never come?". . . .The parallel in this poem between playing football and serving in the Army reflects the recruiting drives that had been made at football matches earlier in the war. The Imperial War Museum preserves the following rather amateur poster: "Men of Millwall / Hundreds of Football enthusiasts / are joining the Army daily. / Don't be left behind. / Let the Enemy hear the 'LION'S ROAR'. Join and be in at THE FINAL / and give them a / KICK OFF THE EARTH".' ('Some Contemporary Allusions in Poems by Rosenberg, Owen and Sassoon', N&Q, n.s., xxvi, no. 4 [August 1979], 333)

CP&F, 351

A TERRE
(being the philosophy of many soldiers)

Sit on the bed. I'm blind, and three parts shell.
Be careful; can't shake hands now; never shall.
Both arms have mutinied against me, – brutes.
My fingers fidget like ten idle brats.

5   I tried to peg out soldierly, – no use!
One dies of war like any old disease.
This bandage feels like pennies on my eyes.
I have my medals? – Discs to make eyes close.
My glorious ribbons? – Ripped from my own back
10 In scarlet shreds. (That's for your poetry book.)

A short life and a merry one, my buck!
We used to say we'd hate to live dead-old, –
Yet now . . . I'd willingly be puffy, bald,
And patriotic. Buffers catch from boys
15 At least the jokes hurled at them. I suppose
Little I'd ever teach a son, but hitting,
Shooting, war, hunting, all the arts of hurting.
Well, that's what I learnt, – that, and making money.

Your fifty years ahead seem none too many?
20 Tell me how long I've got? God! For one year
To help myself to nothing more than air!
One Spring! Is one too good to spare, too long?
Spring wind would work its own way to my lung,
And grow me legs as quick as lilac-shoots.

25 My servant's lamed, but listen how he shouts!
When I'm lugged out, he'll still be good for that.
Here in this mummy-case, you know, I've thought
How well I might have swept his floors for ever.
I'd ask no nights off when the bustle's over,
30 Enjoying so the dirt. Who's prejudiced
Against a grimed hand when his own's quite dust,
Less live than specks that in the sun-shafts turn,
Less warm than dust that mixes with arms' tan?

I'd love to be a sweep, now, black as Town,
35 Yes, or a muckman. Must I be his load?

O Life, Life, let me breathe, – a dug-out rat!
Not worse than ours the lives rats lead –
Nosing along at night down some safe rut,
They find a shell-proof home before they rot.
40 Dead men may envy living mites in cheese,
Or good germs even. Microbes have their joys,
And subdivide, and never come to death.
Certainly flowers have the easiest time on earth.
'I shall be one with nature, herb, and stone,'
45 Shelley would tell me. Shelley would be stunned:
The dullest Tommy hugs that fancy now.
'Pushing up daisies' is their creed, you know.

To grain, then, go my fat, to buds my sap,
For all the usefulness there is in soap.
50 D'you think the Boche will ever stew man-soup?
Some day, no doubt, if . . .
                              Friend, be very sure
I shall be better off with plants that share
More peaceably the meadow and the shower.
Soft rains will touch me, – as they could touch once,
55 And nothing but the sun shall make me ware.
Your guns may crash around me. I'll not hear;
Or, if I wince, I shall not know I wince.

Don't take my soul's poor comfort for your jest.
Soldiers may grow a soul when turned to fronds,
60 But here the thing's best left at home with friends.

My soul's a little grief, grappling your chest,
To climb your throat on sobs; easily chased
On other sighs and wiped by fresher winds.

Carry my crying spirit till it's weaned
65 To do without what blood remained these wounds.

Begun at Scarborough in December 1917 (WO, 248), and revised there in July 1918. On 3 December 1917 WO told SO: 'I finished an important poem this afternoon' (CL, 513), and three days later he wrote to SS: 'This "Wild with all Regrets" was begun & ended two days ago, at one gasp. If simplicity, if imaginativeness, if sympathy, if resonance of vowels, make poetry I have not succeeded. But if you say "Here is poetry," it will be so for me. What do you think of my Vowel-rime stunt in this, and "Vision"? Do you consider the hop from <u>Flea</u> to Soul too abrupt?' (CL, 514) At Ripon, in April 1918, 'Wild with all Regrets' was expanded into 'A Terre'.

> 7 pennies: It was once customary to place coins on the eyelids of a corpse to keep them closed.

13–14 Cp. SS, 'Base Details', ll. 1–4:
>> If I were fierce, and bald, and short of breath,
>>> I'd live with scarlet Majors at the Base,
>> And speed glum heroes up the line to death.
>>> You'd see me with my puffy petulant face. . .

> 19 Cp. A. E. Housman, 'Loveliest of trees, the cherry now', ll. 9–12:
>> And since to look at things in bloom
>> Fifty springs are little room,
>> About the woodlands I will go
>> To see the cherry hung with snow.

> 30 dirt: Cp. 'Inspection' (p. 72), l. 8: '"Well, blood is dirt," I said.'

> 34 sweep: chimney-sweep.

> 36 Cp. *King Lear*, v. iii. 307–8: 'Why should a dog, a horse, a rat, have life, / And thou no breath at all?'

> 37 lives: Previous editors read 'existences', but see CP&F, 354.

> 44 The quotation is from Shelley, 'Adonais', xlii:
>> He is made one with Nature: there is heard
>> His voice in all her music, from the moan
>> Of thunder, to the song of night's sweet bird;
>> He is a presence to be felt and known
>> In darkness and in light, from herb and stone,
>> Spreading itself where'er that Power may move
>> Which has withdrawn his being to its own . . .

> 47 'Pushing up daisies': A common slang expression, meaning dead.

48–50 Cp. SS, 'The Tombstone-Maker', ll. 11–12: 'I told him with a sympathetic grin, / That Germans boil dead soldiers down for fat.'

> 54–5 Cp. 'Futility' (p. 135), ll. 1–2: 'Move him into the sun – / Gently its touch awoke him once.'

> 59 Cp. 'Miners' (p. 112), l. 7: 'Frond-forests'.

CP&F, 354

THE KIND GHOSTS

She sleeps on soft, last breaths; but no ghost looms
Out of the stillness of her palace wall,
Her wall of boys on boys and dooms on dooms.

She dreams of golden gardens and sweet glooms,
5   Not marvelling why her roses never fall
Nor what red mouths were torn to make their blooms.

The shades keep down which well might roam her hall.
Quiet their blood lies in her crimson rooms
And she is not afraid of their footfall.

10   They move not from her tapestries, their pall,
Nor pace her terraces, their hecatombs,
Lest aught she be disturbed, or grieved at all.

Revised – it may have been written earlier – at Scarborough on 30 July 1918,
according to the dated MS, this may be the poem referred to in WO's letter to
SO of 8 August 1918 (CL, 567).

     1 She: Probably Britannia. DH notes that 'The word "Brittannia" (Owen's
       spelling was erratic) appears unexplained in a rough list of titles which he
       jotted down that summer; it seems likely to have been a draft title for this
       poem. Compare Swinburne's "Perinde ac Cadaver". While he was in
       France he acquired a copy of Swinburne's *Poems and Ballads*; it was
       probably the last book he read' (*Wilfred Owen* [Writers and Their Work,
       1975], 35).
   11 hecatombs: 'great public sacrifices' (*OED*). WO may have meant 'places
       of great public sacrifice'. Alternatively, he may have used the word,
       incorrectly, to mean 'tombs' or confused it with 'catacombs'.

CP&F, 357

SOLDIER'S DREAM

I dreamed kind Jesus fouled the big-gun gears;
And caused a permanent stoppage in all bolts;
And buckled with a smile Mausers and Colts;
And rusted every bayonet with His tears.

5   And there were no more bombs, of ours or Theirs,
Not even an old flint-lock, nor even a pikel.
But God was vexed, and gave all power to Michael;
And when I woke he'd seen to our repairs.

Begun at Craiglockhart in October 1917 and revised at Scarborough, probably
that November and in July–August 1918. On 27 November 1917, WO wrote to
SS: 'I trust you'll like the "Soldier's Dream" well enough to pass it on to the
Nation or Cambridge? This was the last piece from Craiglockhart.' (CL, 512)

    3 Mausers and Colts: German and American brands of revolver.
    6 flint-lock: Old-fashioned gun with a flint in the hammer for striking a
       spark to ignite a charge of gunpowder.
       pikel: 'hay-fork or pitchfork' (*OED*), but perhaps here meant to suggest
       'bayonet'.
    7 Michael: The Archangel commanding the heavenly armies.

CP&F, 358

[I AM THE GHOST OF SHADWELL STAIR]

I am the ghost of Shadwell Stair.
  Along the wharves by the water-house,
  And through the cavernous slaughter-house,
I am the shadow that walks there.

5 Yet I have flesh both firm and cool,
  And eyes tumultuous as the gems
  Of moons and lamps in the full Thames
When dusk sails wavering down the Pool.

Shuddering, a purple street-arc burns
10 Where I watch always. From the banks
  Dolorously the shipping clanks.
And after me a strange tide turns.

I walk till the stars of London wane,
  And dawn creeps up the Shadwell Stair.
15 But when the crowing sirens blare,
I with another ghost am lain.

Drafted at Scarborough in January–February 1918, and revised there in
July–August 1918, this poem, as DH notes, 'bears a marked similarity to Oscar
Wilde's *Impression du Matin* and may have been a deliberate imitation. Shadwell
Dock Stair is one of the many flights of steps leading from quay to water's edge
along that part of the Thames known as the Pool of London.' (DH, 113)

  3 cavernous: Previous editors read 'dripping'.
  7 full: Previous editors read 'lapping'.
  12 Bäckman suggests (62) that the ghost is that of a prostitute after whom 'a
    strange tide [of men] turns'. The ghost may, indeed, have been intended to
    be that of the specific prostitute 'With lips of flame and heart of stone' in
    Wilde's poem.

CP&F, 360

ELEGY IN APRIL AND SEPTEMBER
(jabbered among the trees)

1

Hush, thrush! Hush, missel-thrush, I listen . . .
I heard the flush of footsteps through loose leaves,
And a low whistle by the water's brim.

Still! daffodil! Nay, hail me not so gaily, –
5   Your gay gold lily daunts me and deceives,
Who follow gleams more golden and more slim.

Look, brook! O run and look, O run!
The vain reeds shook? – Yet search till grey sea heaves,
And I will stray among these fields for him.

10   Gaze, daisy! Stare through haze and glare,
And mark the hazardous stars all dawns and eves,
For my eye withers, and his star wanes dim.

2

Close, rose, and droop, heliotrope,
And shudder, hope! The shattering winter blows.
15   Drop, heliotrope, and close, rose . . .

Mourn, corn, and sigh, rye.
Men garner you, but youth's head lies forlorn.
Sigh, rye, and mourn, corn . . .

Brood, wood, and muse, yews,
20   The ways gods use we have not understood.
Muse, yews, and brood, wood . . .

Begun at Ripon in April–May 1918, this attempt at a pastoral elegy was
continued in France the following September. On the back of one MS, WO has
written 'Mat[t]hew Arnold' and beneath that a list beginning 'Thyr[s]is /
Scholar Gipsy'; and it would seem that WO had Arnold's elegies in mind as
models for his own. CDL prints only an earlier version of ll. 1–12.

TITLE The subject of this elegy – in one draft described as 'a Poet . . . reported
      killed' – has not been identified.
    1 missel-thrush: WO wrote (and CDL reproduces his error) 'missen-thrush'.

EXPOSURE

Our brains ache, in the merciless iced east winds that knive us . . .
Wearied we keep awake because the night is silent . . .
Low, drooping flares confuse our memory of the salient . . .
Worried by silence, sentries whisper, curious, nervous,
5   But nothing happens.

Watching, we hear the mad gusts tugging on the wire,
Like twitching agonies of men among its brambles.
Northward, incessantly, the flickering gunnery rumbles,
Far off, like a dull rumour of some other war.
10   What are we doing here?

The poignant misery of dawn begins to grow . . .
We only know war lasts, rain soaks, and clouds sag stormy.
Dawn massing in the east her melancholy army
Attacks once more in ranks on shivering ranks of grey,
15   But nothing happens.

Sudden successive flights of bullets streak the silence.
Less deathly than the air that shudders black with snow,
With sidelong flowing flakes that flock, pause, and renew;
We watch them wandering up and down the wind's nonchalance,
20   But nothing happens.

Pale flakes with fingering stealth come feeling for our faces –
We cringe in holes, back on forgotten dreams, and stare, snow-dazed,
Deep into grassier ditches. So we drowse, sun-dozed,
Littered with blossoms trickling where the blackbird fusses,
25   – Is it that we are dying?

Slowly our ghosts drag home: glimpsing the sunk fires, glozed
With crusted dark-red jewels; crickets jingle there;
For hours the innocent mice rejoice: the house is theirs;
Shutters and doors, all closed: on us the doors are closed, –
30   We turn back to our dying.

Since we believe not otherwise can kind fires burn;
Nor ever suns smile true on child, or field, or fruit.
For God's invincible spring our love is made afraid;
Therefore, not loath, we lie out here; therefore were born,
35   For love of God seems dying.

Tonight, this frost will fasten on this mud and us,
Shrivelling many hands, puckering foreheads crisp.
The burying-party, picks and shovels in shaking grasp,
Pause over half-known faces. All their eyes are ice,
40   But nothing happens.

Begun at Scarborough in December 1917, when one unfinished line was written
at the top of the MS of the fragment 'Cramped in that funnelled hole . . .' (p. 183);
revised there in early 1918; and finished in France in September 1918, when its
final draft was written on the same paper as that used for the second draft of
'Elegy in April and September' (p. 161), which was composed in that
month. WO appears to have dated the final draft of 'Exposure' 'Feb. 1916', but
the '6' could be an imperfect '8' (WO, 246–8). EB suggested that WO may have
intended to write 'Feb. 1917', since the poem stems from experiences described
in a letter to SO dated 4 February 1917. (See DH, 'The Date of Wilfred
Owen's "Exposure"', N&Q, n.s., xxiii, no. 7 [July 1976], 305–8.) On 22 April
1918, WO wrote to SO: 'to quote myself cynically "Nothing happens"' (CL,
548), which suggests that 'Exposure' was far enough advanced for her to be
expected to recognize its refrain. It appears, under the title 'Nothing happens',
in one of the lists of contents drawn up at Ripon between March and June 1918
(see Appendix B).

1 An ironic echo of Keats, 'Ode to a Nightingale', ll. 1–2: 'My heart aches,
and a drowsy numbness pains / My sense.'

3 salient: The front line in places jutted into enemy territory, and at such
'salients' the fighting tended to be fiercest.

9 Cp. Matthew 24:6: 'wars and rumours of wars'; also WO to ELG, 25
July 1915: 'You say you "hear of wars and rumours of wars". *Vous en êtes
là seulement?* You hear Rumours? The rumours, over here, make the ears
of the gunners bleed.' (CL, 349)

14 grey: The German troops wore grey uniforms and, like the dawn, came
from the east.

22 Cp. 'Cramped in that funnelled hole . . .' (p. 183).

23 drowse: See note on l. 1 above.

26 Cp. the song: 'Keep the home fires burning . . . Though your lads are
   far away they dream of home.'
   glozed: A conflation of 'glowing' and 'glazed'.

29 DH, in 'The Date of Wilfred Owen's "Exposure"', suggests a link with
   WO's postcard of 24 November 1917 to SO, in which he describes how
   he found himself at York in the small hours of the morning. The Station
   Hotel was full and 'the other hotels would not open to my knocking'
   (CL, 508).

33 God's invincible spring: Cp. the fragment 'The Wrestlers' (p. 184):
   'And all the ardour of the invincible spring'.

36 SS, EB, and CDL print 'His frost', an attractive but inaccurate reading.

39 All their eyes are ice: Cp. Yeats, 'The Happy Townland', l. 11: 'Queens,
   their eyes blue like the ice'.

CP&F, 365

THE SENTRY

We'd found an old Boche dug-out, and he knew,
And gave us hell; for shell on frantic shell
Lit full on top, but never quite burst through.
Rain, guttering down in waterfalls of slime,
5   Kept slush waist-high and rising hour by hour,
And choked the steps too thick with clay to climb.
What murk of air remained stank old, and sour
With fumes from whizz-bangs, and the smell of men
Who'd lived there years, and left their curse in the den,
10   If not their corpses . . .
                              There we herded from the blast
Of whizz-bangs; but one found our door at last, –
Buffeting eyes and breath, snuffing the candles,
And thud! flump! thud! down the steep steps came thumping
And sploshing in the flood, deluging muck,
15   The sentry's body; then his rifle, handles
Of old Boche bombs, and mud in ruck on ruck.
We dredged it up, for dead, until he whined,
'O sir – my eyes, – I'm blind, – I'm blind, – I'm blind.'
Coaxing, I held a flame against his lids
20   And said if he could see the least blurred light
He was not blind; in time they'd get all right.
'I can't,' he sobbed. Eyeballs, huge-bulged like squids',
Watch my dreams still, – yet I forgot him there
In posting Next for duty, and sending a scout
25   To beg a stretcher somewhere, and flound'ring about
To other posts under the shrieking air.

Those other wretches, how they bled and spewed,
And one who would have drowned himself for good, –
I try not to remember these things now.
30   Let Dread hark back for one word only: how,
Half-listening to that sentry's moans and jumps,
And the wild chattering of his shivered teeth,
Renewed most horribly whenever crumps

Pummelled the roof and slogged the air beneath, –
35 Through the dense din, I say, we heard him shout
'I see your lights!' – But ours had long gone out.

Begun at Craiglockhart between August and October 1917, continued at Scarborough in May 1918, and completed in France that September (WO, 274), this must be one of the 'few poems' that accompanied WO's letter of 22 September 1918 to SS (CL, 578). A year and a half before, on 16 January 1917, he had written to SO: 'In the Platoon on my left the sentries over the dug-out were blown to nothing. One of these poor fellows was my first servant whom I rejected. If I had kept him he would have lived, for servants don't do Sentry Duty. I kept my own sentries half way down the stairs during the more terrific bombardment. In spite of this one lad was blown down and, I am afraid, blinded.' (CL, 428). Previous editors follow an earlier MS.

    8 whizz-bangs: Small shells of such high velocity that the sound made in
       passing through the air is almost simultaneous with the explosion.
    22 Eyeballs: Cp. the other tormented eyes that stare from 'Dulce et
       Decorum Est' (p. 117), l. 19, and 'Greater Love' (p. 143), l. 6.
    25 flound'ring: Cp. letter of 16 January 1917 quoted above: 'I was
       mercifully helped to do my duty and crawl, wade, climb and flounder
       over No Man's Land to visit my other post' (CL, 427–8).
    28 one: Cp. letter quoted above: 'I nearly broke down and let myself drown
       in the water that was now slowly rising over my knees' (CL, 427).

CP&F, 371

Head to limp head, the sunk-eyed wounded scanned
Yesterday's *Mail*; the casualties (typed small)
And (large) Vast Booty from our Latest Haul.
Also, they read of Cheap Homes, not yet planned,
5   'For', said the paper, 'when this war is done
The men's first instincts will be making homes.
Meanwhile their foremost need is aerodromes,
It being certain war has but begun.
Peace would do wrong to our undying dead, –
10 The sons we offered might regret they died
If we got nothing lasting in their stead.
We must be solidly indemnified.
Though all be worthy Victory which all bought,
We rulers sitting in this ancient spot
15 Would wrong our very selves if we forgot
The greatest glory will be theirs who fought,
Who kept this nation in integrity.'
Nation? – The half-limbed readers did not chafe
But smiled at one another curiously
20 Like secret men who know their secret safe.
(This is the thing they know and never speak,
That England one by one had fled to France,
Not many elsewhere now, save under France.)
Pictures of these broad smiles appear each week,
25 And people in whose voice real feeling rings
Say: How they smile! They're happy now, poor things.

Written in France in mid- to late September 1918 (WO, 273–4). On 22
September, WO wrote to SS: 'Did you see what the Minister of Labour said in
the *Mail* the other day? "The first instincts of the men <u>after the cessation of</u>
hostilities will be to return home." And again –
"All classes <u>acknowledge</u> their indebtedness to the soldiers & sailors . . ."
    'About the same day, Clemenceau is reported by the *Times* as saying: "<u>All</u> are
worthy . . . yet we should be untrue to ourselves if we forgot that the <u>greatest</u>
glory will be to the splendid poilus, who, etc."
    'I began a Postscript to these Confessions, but hope you will already have
lashed yourself, (lashed <u>yourself</u>!) into something . . .' (CL, 578) The *Times* of 19
September 1918 had reported the French premier as saying: 'All are worthy of
victory, because they will know how to honour it. Yet, however, in the ancient

spot where sit the fathers of the Republic we should be untrue to ourselves if we forgot that the greatest glory will be to those splendid *poilus* [French slang for 'common soldiers'] who will see confirmed by history the titles of nobility which they themselves have earned. At the present moment they ask for nothing more than to be allowed to complete the great work which will assure them of immortality. What do they want and what do you? To keep on fighting victoriously until the moment when the enemy will understand there is no possible negotiation between crime and right.'

TITLE Taken from one of the most popular British songs on the Western Front, which begins:

> What's the use of worrying?
>   It never was worth while,
> So, pack up your troubles in your old kit-bag
>   And smile, smile, smile.

CP&F, 374

SPRING OFFENSIVE

Halted against the shade of a last hill
They fed, and eased of pack-loads, were at ease;
And leaning on the nearest chest or knees
Carelessly slept.
     But many there stood still
5 To face the stark blank sky beyond the ridge,
Knowing their feet had come to the end of the world.
Marvelling they stood, and watched the long grass swirled
By the May breeze, murmurous with wasp and midge;
And though the summer oozed into their veins
10 Like an injected drug for their bodies' pains,
Sharp on their souls hung the imminent ridge of grass,
Fearfully flashed the sky's mysterious glass.

Hour after hour they ponder the warm field
And the far valley behind, where buttercups
15 Had blessed with gold their slow boots coming up;
When even the little brambles would not yield
But clutched and clung to them like sorrowing arms.
They breathe like trees unstirred.

Till like a cold gust thrills the little word
20 At which each body and its soul begird
And tighten them for battle. No alarms
Of bugles, no high flags, no clamorous haste, –
Only a lift and flare of eyes that faced
The sun, like a friend with whom their love is done.
25 O larger shone that smile against the sun, –
Mightier than his whose bounty these have spurned.

So, soon they topped the hill, and raced together
Over an open stretch of herb and heather
Exposed. And instantly the whole sky burned
30 With fury against them; earth set sudden cups
In thousands for their blood; and the green slope
Chasmed and deepened sheer to infinite space.

Of them who running on that last high place

Breasted the surf of bullets, or went up
On the hot blast and fury of hell's upsurge,
Or plunged and fell away past this world's verge,
Some say God caught them even before they fell.

But what say such as from existence' brink
Ventured but drave too swift to sink,
The few who rushed in the body to enter hell,
And there out-fiending all its fiends and flames
With superhuman inhumanities,
Long-famous glories, immemorial shames –
And crawling slowly back, have by degrees
Regained cool peaceful air in wonder –
Why speak not they of comrades that went under?

Begun probably at Scarborough in July 1918, this poem was revised in France in mid- to late September (WO, 274–6). A fair copy of ll. 1–17 was sent with WO's letter of 22 September 1918 to SS. An accompanying note asked: 'Is this worth going on with? I don't want to write anything to which a soldier would say No Compris!' (CU) There is no evidence that SS replied. The poem draws on WO's experience of the Allies' 'spring offensive' in April 1917 (WO, 178–82), and its MSS show that it was never finally revised.

2–3   Previous editors read: 'They fed, and lying easy, were at ease / And, finding comfortable chests and knees,'

11   ridge: Previous editors read 'line'.

14–15   buttercups: Previous editors read 'the buttercup'. WO had coined the image of l. 15 in 1907, returning through the fields to Shrewsbury after Evensong in Uffington Church. HO remembered: 'Wilfred gently pressed my arm for silence – hesitated a moment and then called quietly back, "Harold's boots are blessed with gold"' (JFO, I. 176). The image subsequently appeared in 'A Palinode' (p. 54), ll. 17–20:
    But if the sovereign sun I might behold
    With condescension coming down benign,
    And blessing all the field and air with gold,
    Then the contentment of the world was mine.
Cp. also Keats, 'To Autumn', ll. 2–4:
    Close bosom-friend of the maturing sun;
    Conspiring with him how to load and bless
    With fruit the vines that round the thatch-eaves run. . . .

16   When: Previous editors read 'Where'.

17   arms: Previous editors read 'hands'.

18 The MS reads: '~~All they strange day~~ they breathe like trees unstirred', and one must suppose that WO intended to find alternatives for the cancelled words.

23–5 Cp. WO to CO, 14 May 1917: 'And his face shone with the brightness of the sun' (CL, 459).

29–31 Cp. Henri Barbusse, *Under Fire* (1917), 244: 'Abruptly, across all the width of the opposite slope, lurid flames burst forth that strike the air with terrible detonations. In line from left to right fires emerge from the sky and explosions from the ground.'

30 DH notes 'The word *cups* suggests not only shell-holes but also *buttercup[s]* (l. 14) and chalices, cups which are used in the Mass to contain the wine which is both a blessing (cf. *blessed with gold*) and sacrificial blood. Having refused the offered blessing of communion with the natural order, the men have become victims sacrificed to an outraged Nature.' (DH, 135) Dr Ellen Sarot has detected an echo of Genesis 4: 10–11: 'The voice of thy brother's blood crieth unto me from the ground. And now art thou cursed from the earth, which hath opened her mouth to receive thy brother's blood from thy hand. . . .'

33 last high place: 'another reference to sacrifice – hilltop sacrificial altars were known in ancient times as "high places"' (DH, 135).

34 Previous editors read: 'Leapt to swift unseen bullets, or went up'. EB misread 'surf' as 'swift'. Of the variant, and mainly cancelled, forms of this line (see transcript on CP&F, 378), I prefer one first proposed by Welland.

CP&F, 376

THE FRAGMENTS

[FULL SPRINGS OF THOUGHT]

Extracts from this verse letter are quoted in the Memoir prefacing EB, *but as the whereabouts of the MS have long been unknown, I reproduce EB's text, with his commentary in italic.*

One warm day in December 1911 he wrote a letter in verse, from somewhere in Oxfordshire.

Full springs of Thought around me rise
Like Rivers Four to water my fair garden.
1 Eastwards, where lie wide woodlands, rich as Arden,
From out the beechen solitudes hath sprung
A stream of verse from aerial Shelley's tongue,
While, as he drifted on between the banks
2 Of happy Thames, the waters 'neath the planks
Of his light boat gurgled contentedly
And ever with his dreams kept company.
Today, the music of the slow, turmoiling river,
The music of the rapid vision-giver,
To me are vocal both.
     To eastward, too,
A churchyard sleeps, and one infirm old yew,
Where in the shadows of the fading day,
3 Musing on faded lives, sate solemn Gray.
There to majestic utterance his soul was wrought,
And still his mighty chant is fraught
With golden teaching for the world, and speaks
Strong things with sweetness unto whoso seeks.
Yet can I never sit low at his feet
And, questioning, a gracious answer meet.
For he is gone, and his high dignity
Lost in the past (tho' he may haply be
Far in Futurity as well).
     To north
4 Are hills where Arnold wandered forth
Which, like his verse, still undulate in calm
And tempered beauty.
     And the marriage-psalm
5 Was sung o'er Tennyson, small space away.

*This rhyming letter has something still more intimate, for, towards
its close, Owen declares his longing for a new great poet – for all of
us, and himself:*

Let me attain

To talk with him, and share his confidence.

*His loneliness as a young poet breaks out; he may read even Keats and
'still', he appeals, 'I am alone among the Unseen Voices'.*

Written, probably at Dunsden, in December 1911 (CL, 593).

1 At one time a large forest in the Midlands, centred on Warwickshire, Arden is
  the scene of much of the action in *As You Like It*.
2 Shelley rowed up the Thames to Lechlade, Gloucestershire, in 1815.
3 Gray conceived his 'Elegy in a Country Churchyard' in that of Stoke Poges,
  Buckinghamshire, the village where he completed his poem in 1750.
4 Cumnor Hill on the outskirts of Oxford features in Arnold's poem 'The
  Scholar-Gipsy'.
5 Tennyson married Emily Sellwood in the church of the village of Shiplake,
  Oxfordshire, in 1850.

[AN IMPERIAL ELEGY]

1   Not one corner of a foreign field
    But a span as wide as Europe;
    An appearance of a titan's grave,
    And the length thereof a thousand miles,
    It crossed all Europe like a mystic road,
    Or as the Spirits' Pathway lieth on the night.
    And I heard a voice crying
2   This is the Path of Glory.

Written sometime between September 1915 and the early summer of 1916. The fragment 'Purgatorial Passions' (CP&F, 455), which is on identical paper, carries a marginal note, 'How to Instruct in Aiming and Firing', the title of a military manual, which suggests that this fragment was written during one of the musketry courses WO took in 1916. On 1 August 1914 he had told SO: 'I made the mistake the other day, of striking the opening bars of *Marche Funèbre*; since when [Nénette Léger] pesters me daily for more' (CL, 272). EB, 122; CDL.

1 Cp. Rupert Brooke, 'The Soldier', l. 2: 'there's some corner of a foreign field'. WO owned a copy of Brooke's *1914 & Other Poems* (13th imp., 1916).
2 Cp. Gray, 'Elegy Written in a Country Churchyard', l. 36: 'The paths of glory lead but to the grave.'

CP&F, 454

[I KNOW THE MUSIC]

1   All sounds have been as music to my listening:
2   Pacific lamentations of slow bells,
    The crunch of boots on blue snow rosy-glistening,
        Shuffle of autumn leaves; and all farewells:

3   Bugles that sadden all the evening air,
        And country bells clamouring their last appeals
    Before [the] music of the evening prayer;
4   Bridges, sonorous under carriage wheels.

    Gurgle of sluicing surge through hollow rocks,
        The gluttonous lapping of the waves on weeds,
    Whisper of grass; the myriad-tinkling flocks,
        The warbling drawl of flutes and shepherds' reeds.

    The orchestral noises of October nights
        Blowing [   ] symphonetic storms
    Of startled clarions [   ]
        Drums, rumbling and rolling thunderous and [   ].

    Thrilling of throstles in the keen blue dawn,
5   Bees fumbling and fuming over sainfoin-fields.

Written at Craiglockhart in late August or early September 1917, this fragmentary
poem would seem to owe its catalogue structure to Rupert Brooke, 'The Great
Lover' (quoted in WO to SO, 18 March 1917 [CL, 443]), and may have been
abandoned after WO had drawn on its diction for 'Anthem for Doomed Youth'
(p. 76). EB, CDL, DH.

1   Cp. SS, 'Alone', ll. 1–2: 'I've listened: and all the sounds I heard / Were music.'
2   Cp. 'A Palinode' (p. 54), l. 45: 'Pacific lamentations of a bell', and Flaubert,
    Madame Bovary, part II, chap. VI: 'et la cloche, sonnant toujours, continuait dans
    les airs sa lamentation pacifique'.
3   Cp. 'Anthem for Doomed Youth', l. 8: 'And bugles calling for them from sad
    shires'.
4   Cp. 'A Palinode', l. 44: 'Bridges, sonorous under rapid wheels'.
5   sainfoin: a herb grown for fodder.

CP&F, 485–6

[BUT I WAS LOOKING AT THE PERMANENT STARS]

1   Bugles sang, saddening the evening air,
And bugles answered, sorrowful to hear.

Voices of boys were by the river-side.
Sleep mothered them; and left the twilight sad.
The shadow of the morrow weighed on men.

Voices of old despondency resigned,
Bowed by the shadow of the morrow, slept.

[   ] dying tone
Of receding voices that will not return.
The wailing of the high far-travelling shells
And the deep cursing of the provoking [   ].

2   The monstrous anger of our taciturn guns.
The majesty of the insults of their mouths.

Written at Craiglockhart in late August 1917 shortly before WO read the
anonymous Prefatory Note to *Poems of Today: an Anthology* (1916), that triggered
'Anthem for Doomed Youth' (p. 76), for which poem these fragments may almost
be considered preliminary drafts. EB (entitled 'Voices'), CDL, DH (both entitled
'Bugles Sang').

1 Cp. the fragment, 'I know the music' (p. 178): 'Bugles that sadden all the evening
air'; also 'Anthem for Doomed Youth', l. 8: 'And bugles calling for them from sad
shires'.
2 Cp. 'Anthem for Doomed Youth', l. 2: '– Only the monstrous anger of the guns'.

CP&F, 487–8

BEAUTY

The beautiful, the fair, the elegant,
1 Is that which pleases us, says Kant,
Without a thought of interest or advantage.

I used to watch men when they spoke of beauty
And measure their enthusiasm. One
An old man, seeing a [   ] setting sun,
Praised it [   ] a certain sense of duty
To the calm evening and his time of life.
I know another man that never says a Beauty
But of a horse; [   ]

Men seldom speak of beauty, beauty as such,
Not even lovers think about it much.
Women of course consider it for hours
In mirrors; [   ]

A shrapnel ball –
Just where the wet skin glistened when he swam –
Like a full-opened sea-anemone.
2 We both said 'What a beauty! What a beauty, lad!'
I knew that in that flower he saw a hope
Of living on, and seeing again the roses of his home.
Beauty is that which pleases and delights,
Not bringing personal advantage – Kant.
But later on I heard
A canker worked into that crimson flower
And that he sank with it
And laid it with the anemones off Dover.

Written at Craiglockhart, probably in September 1917. WO may have been
remembering an event described in his letter of 6 [?8] April 1917 to SO:
'Another night I was putting out an Advanced Post when we were seen or
heard and greeted with Shrapnel. The man crouching shoulder to shoulder to
me gets a beautiful round hole deep in his biceps.' (CL, 450) EB (Notes, 129),
CDL.

1 Cp. Immanuel Kant, *The Critique of Judgement* (trans. James Creed
Meredith, Oxford, 1928), l. i. i, 'Analytic of the Beautiful', First Moment, 5:

A vague pearl, a wan pearl
You showed me once; I peered through far-gone winters
Until my mind was fog-bound in that gem.

Blue diamonds, cold diamonds
You shook before me, so that out of them
Glittered and glowed vast diamond dawns of spring.

Tiger-eyed rubies, wrathful rubies
You rolled. I watched their hot hearts fling
Flames from each glaring summer of my life.

Quiet amber, mellow amber
You lifted; and behold the whole air rife
With evening, and the auburn autumn cloud.

But pale skin, your pearl skin
Show this to me, and I shall have surprise
Of every snow-lit dawn before it break.

But clear eyes, your fresh eyes
Open; that I may laugh, and lightly take
All air of early April in one hour.

But brown curls, O shadow me with curls,
Full of September mist, half-gleam, half-glower,
And I shall roam warm nights in lands far south.

'The *agreeable* is what GRATIFIES a man; the *beautiful* what simply PLEASES
him; the *good* what is ESTEEMED (approved), i.e. that on which he sets an
objective worth. . . . Of all these three kinds of delight, that of taste in the
beautiful may be said to be the one and only disinterested and *free* delight;
for, with it, no interest, whether of sense or reason, extorts approval.'
2 The wound is said to be a beauty because it is seen to be a 'blighty', a
soldiers' slang term for one serious enough for the sufferer to be sent back
to 'Blighty' (England).

CP&F, 489–90

Then in an instant from your mouth
Give me the fury of noondays and the sum
Of the fulness of summers yet to come.

Drafted, probably in mid-November 1917, when WO was staying at the
Regent Palace Hotel (CL, 506–7). He may have abandoned this poem after
drawing on its diction for the more successful one beginning 'I saw his round
mouth's crimson deepen as it fell' (p. 100).

    CDL prints the first three stanzas only.

1 Graham Holliday detects an echo of Keats, 'Had I a man's fair form', l. 14:
'I'll gather some spells, and incantation.'

CP&F, 494–6

[CRAMPED IN THAT FUNNELLED HOLE]

1 Cramped in that funnelled hole, they watched the dawn
   Open a jagged rim around; a yawn
   Of death's jaws, which had all but swallowed them
2 Stuck in the bottom of his throat of phlegm.

3 They were in one of many mouths of Hell
   Not seen of seers in visions; only felt
   As teeth of traps; when bones and the dead are smelt
   Under the mud where long ago they fell
   Mixed with the sour sharp odour of the shell.

Written at Scarborough, probably on 4 December 1917. The previous day WO
had written to SO: 'I'm going to get up at dawn tomorrow to do a dawn piece
which I've had in mind since those dismal hours at York, 3 to 7 a.m.! All
dressed up, and nowhere to go.' (CL, 513) (See DH, 'The Date of Wilfred
Owen's "Exposure"', N&Q, n.s., xxiii, no. 7 [July 1976], 305–8, for a discussion
of the linked roots of that poem and this.) 'Cramped in that funnelled hole'
was prompted by WO's reading of Tennyson (WO, 248 and 321) and Barbusse
(CL, 520). Like such other of WO's visions of the descent into Hell as 'Deep
under turfy grass and heavy clay' (p. 39), 'Uriconium' (p. 42), and 'The Show'
(p. 132), the hole or tunnel is described in physical terms. EB, CDL, DH.

1 Cp. 'Mental Cases' (p. 146), l. 22: 'Dawn breaks open like a wound that
  bleeds afresh.'
2 Cp. Henri Barbusse, *Under Fire* (1917), 126: 'The soldier held his peace. In
  the distance he saw the night as *they* would pass it – cramped up, trembling
  with vigilance in the deep darkness, at the bottom of the listening-hole
  whose ragged jaws showed in black outline all around whenever a gun
  hurled its dawn into the sky.'
3 Cp. Tennyson, 'The Charge of the Light Brigade', ll. 24–6: 'Into the jaws of
  Death, / Into the mouth of Hell / Rode the six hundred.'

CP&F, 511–3

THE WRESTLERS

So neck to neck and obstinate knee to knee
Wrestled those two; and peerless Heracles
Could not prevail nor catch at any vantage;
But those huge hands which small had strangled snakes
Let slip the writhing of Antaeas' wrists;
Those clubs of hands that wrenched the necks of bulls
Now fumbled round the slim Antaeas' limbs
Baffled. Then anger swelled in Heracles,
And terribly he grappled broader arms,
And yet more firmly fixed his grasping feet,
And up his back the muscles bulged and shone
Like climbing banks and domes of towering cloud.
Many who watched that wrestling say he laughed, –
But not so loud as on Eurystheus of old,
But that his pantings, seldom loosed, long pent,
Were like the sighs of lions at their meat.
Men say their fettered fury tightened hour by hour,
Until the veins rose tubrous on their brows
And froth flew thickly-shivered from both beards.
As pythons shudder, bridling-in their spite,
So trembled that Antaeas with held strength,
While Heracles, – the thews and cordage of his thighs
Straitened and strained beyond the utmost stretch
From quivering heel to haunch like sweating hawsers –
But only staggered backward. Then his throat
Growled, like a great beast when his meat is touched,
As if he smelt some guile behind Antaeas,
And knew the buttressed bulking of his shoulders
Bore not the mass to move it one thumb's length.
But what it was so helped the man none guessed,
Save Hylas, whom the fauns had once made wise
How earth herself empowered him by her touch,
Gave him the grip and stringency of winter,
And all the ardour of the invincible spring;
How all the blood of June glutted his heart;
And the wild glow of huge autumnal storms
Stirred on his face, and flickered from his eyes;
How, too, Poseidon blessed him fatherly

[184]

With wafts of vigour from the keen sea waves,
And with the subtle coil of currents –
Strange underflows, that maddened Heracles.
And towards the night they sundered, neither thrown.
Whereat came Hylas running to his friend
With fans, and sponges in a laving-bowl,
And brimmed his lord the beakerful he loved,
Which Heracles took roughly, even from him.
Then spake that other from the place he stood:
'O Heracles, I know thy fights and labours,
What man thou wert, and what thou art become,
The lord of strength, queller of perilous monsters,
Hero of heroes, worthy immortal worship,
But me thou canst not quell. For I, I come
Of Earth, and to my father Poseidon,
Whose strength ye know, and whose displeasure ye know.
Therefore be wise, and try me not again,
But say thou findst me peer, and more than peer.'
But Heracles, of utter weariness,
Was loath to answer, either yea or nay.
And a cruel murmur rankled through the crowd.
Now he whose knees propped up the head of him,
Over his lord's ear swiftly whispered thus:
'If thou could'st lift the man in air – enough.
His feet suck secret virtue of the earth.
Lift him, and buckle him to thy breast, and win.'
Up sprang the son of Perseus deeply laughing
And ere the crimson of his last long clutch
Had faded from that insolent's throat, again
4   They closed. Then he, the Argonaut,
Remembering how he tore the oaks in Argos,
Bound both his arms about the other's loins
And with a sudden tugging, easily
Rooted him up; and crushed his inmost bones.
Forth to the town he strode, and through the streets,
Bearing the body light as leopard-skins,
And glorious ran the shouting as he strode –
Some say his footfalls made an earthquake there
So that he dropped Antaeas: some say not:
But that he cast him down by Gea's altar

And Gea sent that earthquake for her son,
To rouse him out of death. And lo! he rose,
Alive, and came to Heracles
Who feasted with the people and their King.
And fain would all make place for him
But he would not consent. And Heracles,
Knowing the hate of Hylas for his deeds,
Feasted and slept; and so forgot the man,
And early on the morrow passed with Hylas
Down to the Argo, for the wind was fair.

Drafted at Craiglockhart in July 1917, in response to a suggestion by Dr Arthur John Brock, one of the three medical officers at the hospital (wo, 196–7). Under the pseudonym 'Arcturus', he wrote an article for *The Hydra* (January 1918), entitled 'Antaeus, or Back to the Land', which ended: 'Antaeus was a young Libyan giant, whose parents were Gaia and Poseidon, Earth and Sea. In a wrestling combat he could not be overthrown as long as his feet were on his Mother Earth. When he was raised off the earth his strength rapidly failed, only to be renewed again at the first contact with the soil. Finally, Hercules, seeing this, lifted him bodily up in the air, and holding him there, crushed him to death in his arms.

'Now surely every officer who comes to Craiglockhart recognises that, in a way, he is himself Antaeus who has been taken from his Mother Earth and well-nigh crushed to death by the war giant or military machine. . . . Antaeus typifies the occupation cure at Craiglockhart. His story is the justification of our activities.'

On [?14] July 1917, WO wrote to SO: 'On the Hercules-Antaeus Subject – there are only 3 or 4 lines in the Dictionaries. So I shall just do a Sonnet' (CL, 476). On the 17th, he incorporated 14 lines from the poem in another letter to SO, adding: 'About 50 lines are now done' (CL, 477). Some days later, he wrote to ELG: 'last week I wrote (to order) a strong bit of Blank: on <u>Antaeus v. Heracles.</u> These are the best lines, methinks: (N.B. Antaeus deriving strength from his Mother Earth nearly licked old Herk.)

> . . . How Earth herself empowered him with her touch,
> Gave him the grip and stringency of winter,
> And all the ardour of th' invincible Spring;
> How all the blood of June glutted his heart.
> And all the glow of huge autumnal storms
> Stirred on his face, and flickered from his eyes.'

(CL, 478)

Brock's article on Antaeus in *The Hydra* is followed by the editorial announcement that 'our late Editor, Mr Owen, has reduced the Antaeus saga to blank verse. This poem we hope to print in our next number'. On 20 December 1917, WO had written to SO of a visit to Edinburgh: 'I saw Dr. Brock, whose first word was "Antaeas!" which they want immediately for the next Mag! Shall have to spin it off again while up here' (CL, 517–18). WO's latest revisions date from this time. No copy of the February 1918 issue of *The Hydra* has come to light, but there is no evidence that the poem was ever finished and it seems unlikely to have been published in part during WO's lifetime. (See DH, 'A Sociological Cure for Shellshock: Dr Brock and Wilfred Owen', *Sociological Review*, XXV, no. 2 [May 1977], 377–86, for a perceptive discussion of Brock's influence on WO in general, and on this poem in particular.) CDL, DH (both print only the 14 lines incorporated in WO's letter of 17 July 1917).

1 Seeking purification for killing his wife and children, Herakles (or Hercules) spent 12 years at the court of King Eurystheus of Tiryns, during which time he performed 12 arduous labours.
2 Hylas, a beautiful youth, was a favourite companion of Herakles. WO wrote 'fawns', almost certainly a misspelling of 'fauns' (as in 'Miners' (p. 112), l. 8.).
3 Cp. 'Exposure' (p. 162), l. 33: 'For God's invincible spring our love is made afraid.'
4 Herakles was an Argonaut, one of the band of heroes that sailed with Jason in the *Argo* in search of the Golden Fleece.

CP&F, 520–5

WILD WITH ALL REGRETS

(To S.S.)

My arms have mutinied against me,—brutes!
My fingers fidget like ten idle brats,
My back's been stiff for hours, damned hours.
Death never gives his squad a Stand-at-ease.
I can't read. There: it's no use. Take your book.
A short life and a merry one, my buck!
We said we'd hate to grow dead-old. But now,
Not to live old seems awful: not to renew
My boyhood with my boys, and teach 'em hitting,
Shooting and hunting,—and all the arts of hurting!
—Well, that's what I learnt. That, and making money.
Your fifty years in store seem none too many,
But I've five minutes. God! For just two years
To help myself to this good air of yours!
One Spring! Is one too hard to spare? Too long?
Spring air would find its own way to my lung,
And grow me legs as quick as lilac-shoots.

*   *   *

Yes, there's the orderly. He'll change the sheets
When I'm lugged out. Oh, couldn't I do that?
Here in this coffin of a bed, I've thought
I'd like to kneel and sweep his floors for ever,—
And ask no nights off when the bustle's over,
For I'd enjoy the dirt. Who's prejudiced
Against a grimed hand when his own's quite dust,—
Less live than specks that in the sun-shafts turn?
Dear dust—in rooms, on roads, on faces' tan!
I'd love to be a sweep's boy, black as Town;
Yes, or a muck-man. Must I be his load?
A flea would do. If one chap wasn't bloody,
Or went stone-cold, I'd find another body.

*   *   *

Which I shan't manage now. Unless it's yours.
I shall stay in you, friend, for some few hours.
You'll feel my heavy spirit chill your chest,
And climb your throat, on sobs, until it's chased
On sighs, and wiped from off your lips by wind.
I think on your rich breathing, brother, I'll be weaned
To do without what blood remained me from my wound.

Written at Scarborough on 5 December 1917 this poem was expanded into 'A
Terre', pp. 155. SS, EB, CDL.

1 Cp. Tennyson, 'Tears, idle tears, I know not what they mean', ll. 19–20:
   'Deep as first love, and wild with all regret;/O Death in Life, the days that
   are no more.'
2 On the MS, the dedication to Siegfried Sassoon is followed by an asterisk.
   A matching asterisk at the foot of the page is followed by the question: 'May
   I?'
3 Cp. A. E. Housman, 'Loveliest of trees, the cherry now', ll.9–12:
      And since to look at things in bloom
      Fifty springs are little room,
      About the woodland I will go
      To see the cherry hung with snow.
4 sweep: chimney-sweep.

CP&F, 355–6

[AS BRONZE MAY BE MUCH BEAUTIFIED]

As bronze may be much beautified
By lying in the dark damp soil,
So men who fade in dust of warfare fade
Fairer, and sorrow blooms their soul.

Like pearls which noble women wear
And, tarnishing, awhile confide
Unto the old salt sea to feed,
Many return more lustrous than they were.

But what of them buried profound,
Buried where we can no more find,
Who [   ]
1   Lie dark for ever under abysmal war?

Written at Scarborough in July 1918, this fragment is a development of another.
EB, CDL, DH.

1   Cp. WO to SS, 1 September 1918: 'Serenity Shelley never dreamed of
    crowns me. Will it last when I shall have gone into Caverns & Abysmals
    such as he never reserved for his worst daemons?' (CL, 571)

CP&F, 529–30

[THE ROADS ALSO]

The roads also have their wistful rest,
When the weather-cocks perch still and roost
And the looks of men turn kind to clocks
1 And the trams go empty to their drome.
     The streets also dream their dreams.

The old houses muse of the old days
And their fond trees lean on them and doze.
On their steps chatter and clatter stops
For the cries of other times hold men
     And they hear the unknown moan.

They remember alien ardours and far futures
And the smiles not seen in happy features.
Their begetters call them from the gutters;
In the gardens unborn child-souls wail,
2   And the dead scribble on walls.

Though their own child cry for them in tears,
Women weep but hear no sound upstairs.
The[y] believe in love they ha[ve] not lived
And passion past the reach of stairs
     To the world's towers or stars.

Written at Scarborough in July–August 1918, this fragment probably owes
something to an experience described in a letter to SO of 18 February 1918:
'Last night I took an artist johnny – called [Emile] Claus . . . to <u>the</u>
Scarborough, where there's not a house built since 1780, not a street much
wider than Claus, and miles of it, mind you, miles of glorious eighteenth
century. It was twilight and the Sunday evening bell.
  'Not a soul in the alleys.
  'Not a lamp lit. A dim moon – and the Past.
  'And we got excited. What excited us, who shall say? We jumped about, we
bumped about, we sang praises, we cursed Manchester; we looked in at half
open doors and blessed the people inside. We saw Shakespeare in a lantern,
and the whole of Italy in a Balcony. A tall chimney became a Greek Column;
and in the inscriptions on the walls we read romances and philosophies.' (CL,
533). EB and CDL print as a poem rather than a fragment. There is an earlier
draft of stanzas 1–3, which those editors conflate with the later.

PREFACE

This book is not about heroes. English poetry is not yet fit to speak of them.

1   Nor is it about deeds, or lands, nor anything about glory, honour, might, majesty, dominion, or power, except War.

Above all I am not concerned with Poetry.

My subject is War, and the pity of War.

The Poetry is in the pity.

2   Yet these elegies are to this generation in no sense consolatory. They may be to the next. All a poet can do today is warn. That is why the true Poets must be truthful.

(If I thought the letter of this book would last, I might have used proper names; but if the spirit of it survives—survives Prussia—my ambition and those names will have achieved fresher fields than Flanders. . . .)

At Ripon, probably in May 1918, WO began this draft Preface for a collection of war poems that he hoped to publish in 1919 (WO, 265–6).

1 Cp. the General Epistle of Jude 25, 'To the only wise God our Saviour, be glory and majesty, dominion and power, both now and ever.'
2 WO had considered – and decided against – calling his book *English Elegies*.

CP&F, 535

---

1 drome: garage.
2 Cp. Blake, 'London', ll. 11–16:
      And the hapless Soldier's sigh
      Runs in blood down Palace walls.

      But most thro' midnight streets I hear
      How the youthful Harlot's curse
      Blasts the new born Infant's tear,
      And blights with plagues the Marriage hearse.

CP&F, 531–2

INDEX OF TITLES AND FIRST LINES

A dismal fog-hoarse siren howls at dawn 139
After the blast of lightning from the east 136
All sounds have been as music to my listening 178
Anthem for Doomed Youth 76
A Poet stood in parley 98
Apologia pro Poemate Meo 101
Arms and the Boy 131
As bronze may be much beautified 190
Asleep 129
As men who call on spirits get response 87
At a Calvary near the Ancre 111
A Terre 155
A thousand suppliants stand around thy throne 3
Autumnal 83
A vague pearl, a wan pearl 181

Ballad of Many Thorns, The 98
Beauty 180
Bent double, like old beggars under sacks 117
Be slowly lifted up, thou long black arm 128
Between the brown hands of a server-lad 86
Budging the sluggard ripples of the Somme 104
Bugles sang, saddening the evening air 179
But I was looking at the permanent stars 179

Calls, The 139
Chances, The 148
Conscious 115
Cramped in that funnelled hole they watched the dawn 183

Daily I muse on her; I muse and fret 41
Dead-Beat, The 121
Deep under turfy grass and heavy clay 39
Disabled 152
Down the close darkening lanes they sang their way 149
Dread of Falling into Naught, The 14
Dulce et Decorum Est 117

Elegy in April and September 161
End, The [After the blast of lightning from the east] 136

Ever again to breathe pure happiness 65
Exposure 162

Far out at sea, the water is as blue 17
Fates, The 64
From my Diary, July 1914 97
Full ninety autumns hath this ancient beech 7
Full springs of Thought around me rise 175
Futility 135

Greater Love 143

Halted against the shade of a last hill 169
Happiness 65
Happy are men who yet before they are killed 122
Has your soul sipped 67
Having, with bold Horatius, stamped her feet 116
Head to limp head, the sunk-eyed wounded scanned 167
He dropped, – more sullenly than wearily 121
He sat in a wheeled chair, waiting for dark 152
His face was charged with beauty as a cloud 60
His fingers wake, and flutter; up the bed 115
Hospital Barge 104
How Do I Love Thee? 63
Hush, thrush! Hush, missel-thrush, I listen 161

I am the ghost of Shadwell Stair 160
I cannot woo thee as the lion his mate 63
I dreamed kind Jesus fouled the big-gun gears 159
If ever I had dreamed of my dead name 73
If it be very strange and sorrowful 83
I have been urged by earnest violins 75
I know the music 178
I leaned, blank-eyed, in lonely thoughtless thought 95
I 'mind as how the night before that show 148
Imperial Elegy, An 177
Impromptu/Now, let me feel the feeling of thy hand 53
Insensibility 122
In Shrewsbury Town e'en Hercules wox tired 62
Inspection 72

In that I loved you, Love, I worshipped you 92
In twos and threes, they have not far to roam 79
I saw his round mouth's crimson deepen as it fell 100
I seldom look into thy brown eyes, child 38
I sometimes think of those pale, perfect faces 80
It lieth low near merry England's heart 42
I, too, saw God through mud 101
It seemed that out of battle I escaped 125
It was a navy boy, so prim, so trim 56

Kind Ghosts, The 158

Last Laugh, The 145
Leaves 97
Le Christianisme 103
Letter, The 114
Let the boy try along this bayonet-blade 131
Lines Written on My Nineteenth Birthday 9
Little Mermaid, The 17
Long ages past in Egypt thou wert worshipped 47

Maundy Thursday 86
Mental Cases 146
Miners 112
Move him into the sun 135
Music 75
My arms have mutinied against me, – brutes! 188
My soul looked down from a vague height, with Death 132
My Shy Hand 110
My shy hand shades a hermitage apart 110

Nay, light me no fire tonight 107
New Heaven, A 59
Next War, The 142
1914 93
Nocturne 52
Not one corner of a foreign field 177
Not this week nor this month dare I lie down 141
Now, as the warm approach of honied slumber blurs my sense 52
Now, let me feel the feeling of thy hand 53
Now slows the beat of Summer's dancing pulse 14

'Oh! Jesus Christ! I'm hit,' he said; and died 145
On a Dream 95
One evening Eros took me by the hand 61
One ever hangs where shelled roads part 111
One knotted a rope with an evil knout 108
One Remains, The 80
On my Songs 90
Our brains ache, in the merciless iced east winds that knive us 162
Out of the endless nave 119
Out there, we walked quite friendly up to Death 142
O World of many worlds, O life of lives 48

Page Eglantine 107
Palinode, A 54
Parable of the Old Man and the Young, The 151
Patting goodbye, doubtless they told the lad 137
Peril of Love, The 87
Perversity 85
Poet in Pain, The 88
Preface 192
Promisers, The 74
Purple 94

Red lips are not so red 143
Rime of the Youthful Mariner, The 108
Roundel/In Shrewsbury Town 62

Schoolmistress 116
Science has looked, and sees no life but this 15
Seeing we never found gay fairyland 59
Send-Off, The 149
Sentry, The 165
She sleeps on soft, last breaths; but no ghost looms 158
Show, The 132
Sing me at dawn but only with your laugh 66
Sit on the bed. I'm blind, and three parts shell 155
S.I.W. 137
Six O'clock in Princes Street 79
Sleeping Beauty, The 81
Smile, Smile, Smile 167

So Abram rose, and clave the wood, and went 151
Sojourning through a southern realm in youth 81
Soldier's Dream 159
Some little while ago, I had a mood 54
Some men sing songs of Pain and scarcely guess 88
So neck to neck and obstinate knee to knee 184
Song of Songs 66
Sonnet/Daily I muse on her 41
Sonnet/On Seeing a Piece of Our Heavy Artillery 128
Sonnet/Written at Teignmouth, on a Pilgrimage to Keats's House 8
So the church Christ was hit and buried 103
Spells and Incantation 181
Spring Offensive 169
Storm 60
Strange Meeting 125
Stunned by their life's explosion into love 96
Suddenly night crushed out the day and hurled 84
Supposed Confessions of a Secondrate Sensitive Mind in Dejection 11
Sweet is your antique body, not yet young 106
Swift, The 69

Tear Song, A 119
The beautiful, the fair, the elegant 180
The browns, the olives, and the yellows died 78
The city lights along the waterside 82
There was a whispering in my hearth 112
The roads also have their wistful rest 191
The time was aeon; and the place all earth 50
They watch me, those informers to the Fates 64
This book is not about heroes 192
Though unseen Poets, many and many a time 90
Three colours have I known the Deep to wear 8
Three rompers run together, hand in hand 91
Time was when I have loved the bards whose strains 11
To —— 91
To Eros 92
To Poesy 3
To the Bitter Sweet-Heart: A Dream 61
Training 141
Two Reflections, The 38

Two Spirits woke me from my sleep this morn 9

Under his helmet, up against his pack 129
Unreturning, The 84
Unto what pinnacles of desperate heights 40
Uriconium 42·

Vividly gloomy, with bright darkling glows 94

War broke: and now the Winter of the world 93
We all love more the Passed and the To Be 85
We'd found an old Boche dug-out, and he knew 165
What passing-bells for these who die as cattle 76
When I awoke, the glancing day looked gay 74
When late I viewed the gardens of rich men 46
When the blue has broken 69
Whereas most women live this difficult life 58
Whither is passed the softly-vanished day 89
Who are these? Why sit they here in twilight 146
Who is the god of Canongate 109
Wild with All Regrets 188
Winter Song 78
With an Identity Disc 73
With B.E.F. June 10. Dear Wife 114
Wrestlers, The 184
Written in a Wood, September 1910 7

'You! What d'you mean by this?' I rapped 72